Reclaiming our lives

Compiled by the FAO Sub-Regional Office for Southern and East Africa. The views expressed in this book do not necessarily reflect the views of FAO.

Published by HSRC Press
Private Bag X9182, Cape Town, 8000, South Africa
www.hsrcpress.ac.za

First published 2006

ISBN 0-7969-2136-9

Cover and book design by Jenny Young
Cover photograph by Kevin Wilson/Africanpictures.net.
The cover photograph is used with permission and should not be taken as any indication of the subject's HIV status.
Production management by Compress
www.compress.co.za | PB2464

Distributed in Africa by Blue Weaver
PO Box 30370, Tokai, Cape Town, 7966, South Africa
Tel: +27 (0) 21 701 4477
Fax: +27 (0) 21 701 7302
email: orders@blueweaver.co.za
www.oneworldbooks.com

Distributed in Europe and the United Kingdom by Eurospan Distribution Services (EDS)
3 Henrietta Street, Covent Garden, London, WC2E 8LU, United Kingdom
Tel: +44 (0) 20 7240 0856
Fax: +44 (0) 20 7379 0609
email: orders@edspubs.co.uk
www.eurospanonline.com

Distributed in North America by Independent Publishers Group (IPG)
Order Department, 814 North Franklin Street, Chicago, IL 60610, USA
Call toll-free: (800) 888 4741
All other enquiries: +1 (312) 337 0747
Fax: +1 (312) 337 5985
email: frontdesk@ipgbook.com
www.ipgbook.com

Reclaiming our lives

HIV and AIDS, women's land and property rights, and livelihoods in southern and East Africa

Narratives and responses

The Global Coalition on Women and AIDS

Contents

Acknowledgements

We would like to thank all the contributors to this book who kindly shared their experiences with us. Sadly, some of these contributors passed away while the manuscript was being drafted. We would also like to thank all the women's organisations and support groups for giving us the opportunity to meet women from their membership. We owe our special thanks to Esther Mwaura-Muiru, Flavia Kyomukama, Sibongile Ndashe, Beatrice Were, Lucy Muguiyi Njuguna, Theresa Makwara, Siphiwe Hlophe, Mary Njeri Kamande, Pelagia Katunzi, Worku Zarai and Lynn Walker. Their initiatives and experiences enriched our knowledge and perspectives for future interventions to support women. Maude Mugisha and Eric Tumwesigye in Uganda provided us with updates on two women's groups living with HIV and AIDS in Uganda and the latest news on Constance and Edivina over the last three years.

We are grateful to Cherryl Walker for her comments and editing, and to Simon Chislett for his patience in managing the production process. Birte Sholtz kindly commented on legal issues affecting women's property rights in the document. Thanks to Angeline Matoushaya, Lalage Katunga and Nelson Marongwe for their assistance and to Ken Dixon for his editing role.

This book is dedicated to Anna Ndonge and Precious Kyarisima,[1] two young widows who passed away in 2004, in the hope that life for their children when they grow up will be better than their mothers' and that they may have a decent shelter to live in, a piece of land to grow food upon and a property of their own.

Kaori Izumi, Ph.D.

Land Tenure and Rural Institutions Officer

FAO Sub-Regional Office for Southern and East Africa

Harare, Zimbabwe, 2006

Acronyms and abbreviations

AIDS	Acquired Immune Deficiency Syndrome
ARVs	Antiretroviral drugs
BRTI	Bio-Medical Research and Training Institute
COHRE	Centre for Housing Rights and Evictions
DART	Development Anti-Retroviral Therapy
FAO	Food and Agriculture Organisation of the United Nations
FOST	Farm Orphan Support Trust of Zimbabwe
GDP	Gross domestic product
GROOTS Kenya	Grassroots Organisations Together in Sisterhood
HIV	Human immunodeficiency virus
JWOP	Justice for Widows and Orphans Project (Zambia)
Ksh.	Kenya shilling
NGO	Non-governmental organisation
OVC	Orphans and vulnerable children
PLWHA	People living with HIV and AIDS
PMTCT	Prevention of Mother to Child Transmission Therapy
RWF	Rwanda Franc
RWN	Rwanda Women's Network
SIDA	Swedish International Development Agency
SWAPOL	Swazis Positive Living
Tsh.	Tanzania shilling
TACAIDS	Tanzania Commission for AIDS
UNAIDS	United Nations AIDS Programme
UNDP	United Nations Development Programme
UNESCO	United Nations Educational, Scientific and Cultural Organisation
UN-HABITAT	United Nations Human Settlements Programme
UNICEF	United Nations Children's Fund
UNFPA	United Nations Population Fund
UNIFEM	United Nations Development Fund for Women
Ush.	Uganda shilling
VSO	Voluntary Services Overseas
VSU	Victim Support Unit (Zambia)
WLC	Women's Legal Centre (South Africa)
WLSA	Women's Law Southern Africa and Education Trust
YWCA	Young Women's Christian Organisation
ZPCDA	Zimbabwe Parents of Children with Disabilities Association
ZWOT	Zimbabwe Widows and Orphans Trust
Z$	Zimbabwean dollar

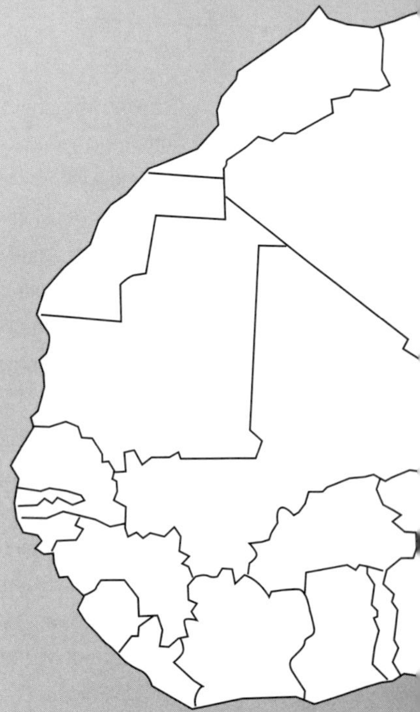

SOUTHERN AND EAST AFRICA

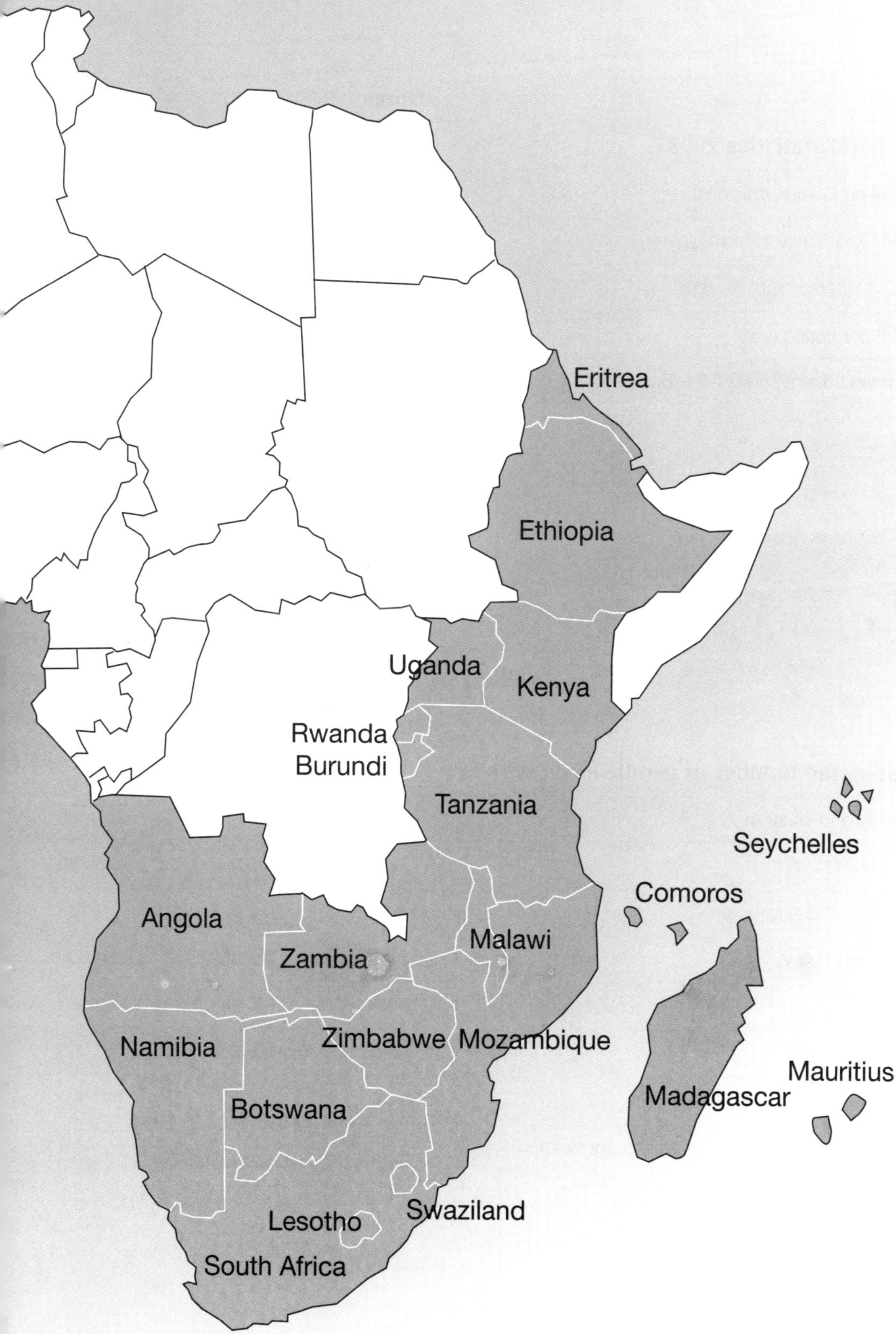

Statistical information by country

General statistics 2003	Eritrea	Kenya	Rwanda
Total population (millions)	4.1	32.7	8.8
Life expectancy at birth (years)	53.8	47.2	43.9
Adult illiteracy rate (% ages 15 +)	43.3	26.4	36.0
GDP per capita (US$)	171	450	195
Human Poverty Index (HPI–1) value (%)	38.7	35.4	37.7

Source: UNDP 2005

HIV and AIDS statistics end 2003

Estimated number of people living with HIV	Eritrea	Kenya	Rwanda
ɩdults and children	60 000	1 200 000	250 000
'ults (15–49)	55 000	1 100 000	230 000
lts (15–49) rate (%)	2.7	6.7	5.1
en (15–49)	31 000	720 000	130 000
ɲn (0–14)	5 600	100 000	22 000
ɜths	6 300	150 000	22 000
ɟue to AIDS (0–17)	39 000	650 000	160 000
ɲnce (%) in young pregnant women ɜpital city	–	–	11.6

2004

South Africa	Swaziland	Tanzania	Uganda	Zambia	Zimbabwe
46.9	1.0	36.9	26.9	11.3	12.9
48.4	32.5	46.0	47.3	37.5	36.9
17.6	20.8	30.6	31.1	32.1	10.0
3 489	1 669	287	249	417	2 443[2]
30.9	52.9	35.8	36.0	46.4	45.9

South Africa	Swaziland	Tanzania	Uganda	Zambia	Zimbabwe
5 300 000	220 000	1 600 000	530 000	920 000	1 800 000
5 100 000	200 000	1 500 000	450 000	830 000	1 600 000
21.5	38.8	8.8	4.1	16.5	24.6
2 900 000	110 000	840 000	270 0000	470 000	930 000
230 000	16 000	140 000	84 000	85 000	120 000
370 000	37 000	160 000	78 000	89 000	170 000
1 100 000	65 000	980 000	940 000	630 000	980 000
24.0 (2002)	39.0 (2002)	7.0 (2002)	10.0 (2002)	22.1 (2001)	– (2002)

( ) indicates the year of the survey

What is needed is real, positive change that will give more power and confidence to women and girls … change that will allow women to play to the full their role in the fight against HIV and AIDS. Empowering women in this struggle must be our strategy for the future.

Kofi A Annan
Secretary-General of the United Nations
1 December 2004

Introduction

HIV and AIDS as an opportunity to advance women's property rights and livelihoods in southern and East Africa.

KAORI IZUMI

Land Tenure and Rural Institutions Officer and HIV and AIDS Focal Point for the FAO Sub-Regional Office for Southern and East Africa, Harare, Zimbabwe.

Overview[3]

This collection of narratives from southern and East Africa aims to raise awareness not only about the heavy impact of HIV and AIDS on women's property rights and livelihoods in the region but also about the active steps being taken by many grassroots organisations to respond to the crisis. Too often, the personal stories of both hardship and resilience in the face of adversity are lost in the statistics and dry overviews of national policies and epidemiological trends. The pandemic is biting deeply into the social fabric of many communities, but it is also galvanising ordinary women and men to respond with compassion and conviction and to organise support groups and innovative ways of defending and promoting the rights of HIV-affected women and children. From this perspective, HIV and AIDS can be seen as an opportunity to expose the immense human cost of discriminatory laws and practices, and point to the social, policy and legislative changes that are necessary if the pandemic is to be combated effectively.

HIV and AIDS in southern and East Africa

It is a well-known fact that women and girls are especially vulnerable to HIV infection. The social group at highest risk is married women, as most HIV infection occurs through external marital relationships conducted by men. In most of the countries in the region, women's access and rights to land and property depend on their relationship to their male family members as a wife, daughter, sister or mother (with some exceptions, especially where a matrilineal kinship system is practised). As more women are educated and earn an independent income, some have managed to acquire land and property in their own right, though such cases are still rare. Women's land and property rights are addressed by some international conventions and by new policies and laws enacted during the course of institutional reforms. However, the gap between formal policy and law and actual practice remains large. One of the major challenges to women's land and property rights in southern and East Africa has been how to bridge the gap between statutory law and customary law, as the latter dominates in practice. Polygamous marriages, involving a mixture of civil marriage and customary marriage, further complicate women's inheritance and property rights, as does the (relatively new) HIV and AIDS pandemic, which is a widow- and orphan-creating disease.

The 2004 UNAIDS Global Report reported that in sub-Saharan Africa, at the end of 2003, 25 million people were estimated to be infected with HIV. Furthermore, 2.2 million adults and children were estimated to have died, leaving 12.1 million orphans (aged between 0 and 17 years). It is anticipated that additional land and property disputes will occur between wives of a polygamous marriage, between widows or orphans and the family members of the deceased, between siblings, and between widows and their children as more men die of AIDS. The inimical nature of the HIV and AIDS disease often puts widows in a vulnerable situation when negotiating inheritance rights, as their health deteriorates and they are forced to endure the social stigmatisation attached to their condition. Therefore, HIV and AIDS further weaken women's and girls' already vulnerable rights relating to land and property.

UN resolutions and initiatives on HIV and AIDS and women's property rights

In 2003, the United Nations adopted two important resolutions on women's property rights. One was the UNHABITAT resolution on 'Women's role and rights in human settlements development and slum upgrading', and the other was the Commission on Human Rights resolution on 'Women's equal ownership, access to, and control over land and equal rights to own property and to adequate housing'. These resolutions recognised the violation of women's property rights as a violation of fundamental human rights and the UN's commitment to prevent such violations. In 2003, the UN Secretary General commissioned a Special Committee on Women, Girls, and HIV and AIDS in Southern Africa, acknowledging that women and girls were the most negatively affected by the HIV and AIDS pandemic. Under this committee, seven key issues were selected for investigation. One of them was HIV and AIDS and the property rights of women and girls.

Although some progress has been made on institutional reform concerning marriage, inheritance and property rights laws, how to apply and enforce such legislation effectively is a key challenge in many countries. Even where progressive laws exist, the state often fails to enforce them. And, while legal reform aimed at protecting and strengthening women's land and property rights should continue, there is also an urgent need to facilitate awareness and understanding of these laws, principally through improving the accessibility of the judicial system to women. At the same time, making new laws an acceptable, normative, and therefore enforceable aspect of communal life presents perhaps the biggest challenge yet.

The momentum generated by liberal, progressive reform needs to be directed towards bringing an end to the suffering of women and children, especially girls, who are often dispossessed of their property, evicted from their homes and land, and thereby forced into destitution, without adequate shelter, food, household effects or livelihoods. Such property-grabbing is not merely a physical stripping of land and property, but is often combined with mental and physical harassment and humiliation of women and children. As a consequence, women and children are left with no land to grow food, no shelter to rest under, no blankets to cover themselves with at night, not even a pot to cook food in. These women and children do not exist in statistics. They are invisible. Property-grabbing from widows and orphans is not a new phenomenon, as such; it existed prior to the HIV and AIDS pandemic. However, HIV and AIDS have, as mentioned above, worsened the situation. Increasing rates of infection and the stigma accompanying the disease only add to the economic vulnerability of widows and orphans.

Many development agencies, including ourselves, that are meant to assist the poorest of the poor, are failing to reach this group of people. This is partly because they are hard to find, but even if they are located, appropriate support systems and procedures are not in place for providing timely assistance.

They are impoverished to the extent that they are not able to seek legal aid and other existing support services, if such exist. HIV and AIDS is an opportunity for us to address and act on the protection, restoration and strengthening of women's property rights, because their devastating impact on the lives of women and children must not be tolerated any longer.

A journey to find survivors of property-grabbing

Since 2000, I have travelled extensively in southern and East Africa and met women and children who have lost land, property, and livelihoods. I have come across several women; most of them widows, many of them HIV-positive, some abandoned, even by their parents, because of their HIV status, and most experiencing land and property disputes with their in-laws, or even with their own sons. I have also met organisations responding creatively to this crisis. This collection of narratives showcases a number of these, which I describe briefly in the remainder of this introduction.

The first group of HIV-positive women I visited was the Bunono-Ihunga Association for Women Living with HIV and AIDS in the Rukungiri district of Uganda. Twenty-four women living positively with HIV and AIDS had formed a support group, started sensitisation on HIV and AIDS at schools and churches, and had initiated a drama group, while also engaging in handicrafts and small livestock projects. Their performance was impressive. The constitution of the group states: 'We are a group of women living positively with HIV. We are determined to look after ourselves and our children while we are still alive.'

When revisited a year later, the group had lost 3 of their 24 members. In 2004, they had lost 3 more, including the youngest widow, Precious Kyarisima, who died at the age of 23 in October. They died of opportunistic diseases such as malaria, primarily due to their inability to access nutritious food and medical treatment. Most of them left behind young children. Another widow from the same group is now bedridden, terminally ill.

Another group I visited in Uganda is called the Sibabinywera Women's Group – Kisasi, Ntinda, Kampala. This is a group of women who were evicted from their rural homes and who lost all their property when their husbands died of HIV and AIDS. The members of this group are all HIV-positive. They are squatters in Kampala without any permanent shelter, surviving by doing casual work, such as cleaning or selling processed food and vegetables. One of the members lost her job as a domestic worker when her employer found out her HIV-positive status. In the case of another group member, working as a cleaner, the place where she cleans during the day is where she sleeps, and then she moves on.

We are losing many more women who could survive if timely and appropriate support such as shelter, basic food, knowledge of nutrition, skills to grow herbs and vegetables, mental and psychosocial support, knowledge of property rights and access to legal support, could be provided. The entire livelihoods of even those women who have managed well can collapse when their health condition deteriorates. The negative effects of HIV and AIDS, poverty, property disputes, harassment by in-laws and mental distress, combine to reduce the status of these women to the extent that they are no longer in control of their own lives. What we are witnessing is a failure of developmental and humanitarian assistance.

Widows are often held responsible for the death of their husbands for allegedly having infected them with HIV and AIDS, or causing their death through witchcraft. There are cases where in-laws deliberately delay a court case involving a property dispute because they believe that the widow will soon die of AIDS. It appears that, for many in-laws, HIV-positive widows are people who are almost dead and do not deserve any semblance of human rights or dignity. The nature and level of humiliation and harassment intensify as a widow's physical, mental and emotional condition declines.

These widows have looked after their bedridden husbands who were dying of HIV and AIDS until the day of their death, selling their belongings to pay medical costs and for funerals. It is the widows who are struggling to look after the children, trying to restore their dignity and survive with whatever meagre means may be left to them.

There are many stories of tragedies, but also of resilience. Despite their painful experiences and memories, there is life after HIV and AIDS and loss of property if the basic support can be provided at the right time. We have seen, too often, how difficult it is for women to get even minimum support before it becomes too late.

Double handicaps and stigma – HIV and AIDS, disability, and poverty

An issue which requires urgent attention is that of HIV and AIDS, disability and poverty. When a child is born disabled, the father often abandons the family, blaming the wife for the disability. Consequently, 90 per cent of the members of the Zimbabwe Parents of Children with Disabilities Association (ZPCDA) are mothers who have been abandoned by their husbands. A recent ZPCDA study shows a high infection rate of HIV and AIDS among the parents of disabled children. According to Theresa Makwara, ZPCDA Co-ordinator, Harare Branch, the Association lost five of its members through HIV- and AIDS-related illnesses between January and May in 2004 alone, making the number of HIV-related deaths among their members 20 in total between 2003 and 2005. This implies that the organisation has lost 5 per cent of its members in two years (the total membership of the ZPCDA Harare branch is approximately 400).

Disabled children are usually sent to their relatives in rural homes when both parents have died or when the father refuses to look after the child following the mother's death. In Zimbabwe, one ten-year-old boy was sent to a village after both parents had died of HIV- and AIDS-related illness. He was kept in a tyre because he was not able to sit on his own. On 28 January 2005, after a short period of time, he died of bed sores.

A little known myth at work in Zimbabwe is that sex with disabled girls cleanses one of HIV and AIDS. This belief is said to have contributed to an increase in the number of cases involving sexual abuse of disabled girls. Because of their disability, many of these girl victims are not able to testify in court. A particularly extreme case involves a family with an HIV-positive mother whose disabled daughter is a victim of sexual abuse, living with the double stigma of disability and HIV, and they have lost shelter, land and property. A multiplicity of actors, including relatives, parents or guardians and society itself, play a role in creating the culture of violence, property-grabbing and general neglect that disabled children are exposed to. If we talk of HIV and AIDS, poverty and the poorest of the poor, we cannot afford to exclude disabled children and their parents.

Women without property – female farm workers

A group usually ignored when discussing women's property rights is female farm workers. For instance, most female farm workers in Zimbabwe are casual workers without any permanent accommodation, vacation leave, health and maternity benefits, pension, gratuities, or retrenchment packages. They have no access to land and own little property. Their vulnerability and poverty often forces them to enter into informal and unstable relationships with men who are permanent farm workers, in order to obtain material support and security. This increases the risk of becoming infected with HIV. Research conducted on 12 farms in the Nyazura farming district, Manicaland, Zimbabwe, and in a nearby town, showed a much higher HIV-infection rate in the commercial farms than the town: 34 per cent for men and 64 per cent for women on the farms, compared to 34 per cent for men and 44 per cent for women in the town (BRTI 2000).

As noted by Lynn Walker, the Director of Farm Orphan Support Trust (FOST) in Zimbabwe from 2000–2005, female farm workers are living on the 'margins of the margins' in terms of their basic rights to property, land, and livelihoods.

Stories of tragedy and resilience

In the course of our journey to find women and children who have lost land, shelter and property, we met a widow whose land was taken by her brother-in-law because she refused to remarry him. She now lives with, in front of her house, 16 graves of relatives which the brother-in-law has buried since 1994. We met a girl orphan who looks after her mentally and physically disabled younger sister, unable to go to school or work because there is nobody to look after the sister. All that the children get is a meal twice a week from a support group. We met 60 girl orphans at a children's training centre, all of whom lost their house and property when their parents died; two of whom were sexually abused by a member of their own family; five of whom were HIV-positive; some of whom were found on the street engaging in commercial sex as a means to raise school fees for their younger siblings. In Zimbabwe, we interviewed a widow whose husband's grave was exhumed by in-laws; relatives who also demolished her house, burned her granary and took all the livestock and inputs she herself had bought through hard work. She was left with the clothes that she wore. There are endless, similar stories.

As I travelled, I was struck by the nature and extent of devastation faced by many women and children, including trauma, poverty and worsening health. The astonishing fact was that the primary supporters of these women and children were women themselves who were in a similar situation: HIV-positive, stripped of property, struggling with poverty, providing home-based care to other people living with HIV and AIDS, with little or no external financial support. What is encouraging is that there are various inspiring initiatives which, however small in scale, provide invaluable assistance to these women and children. Such assistance includes the provision of food and shelter, psychosocial support, furthering property recovery claims and opportunities for economic activity. Considerable numbers of women and children have been helped by these initiatives to overcome trauma and start a new life.

However, there still remains the need to break the vicious cycle of HIV and AIDS, property-grabbing, poverty, commercial sex and further HIV infection.

An outline of the various initiatives we encountered now follows.

Creative initiatives

The Memory Book Project

The Memory Book Project, which originated in Uganda, is a family project aimed at guardians and foster children or parents and their biological children. It provides a simple means of keeping or maintaining details of family and assets together, therefore assuring dependents of sustainable livelihoods in the future. This project teaches the basics on parenting and communication skills to both parents and children, and guardians and foster children. It promotes the disclosure of HIV status of parents to children, and vice versa, and prepares for eventual separation of families in the event of death. It also trains families and children how to handle death when it arrives.

The Memory Book can also act as a tool to reduce the stigma attached to HIV-positive status when this is disclosed. Disclosure without tackling stigma can lead to tragic consequences, as in the case of Gutu Dhlami in South Africa who, in 1994, was stoned to death after disclosing her status. More open discussion, leading to acceptance both within and outside the family, can avoid such extreme situations and lift the burden of secrecy.

The last section of the Memory Book deals with planning for the future, encouraging parents to make wills in order to secure their children's property in the future. In fact, it is a simple way of showing families and children the property belonging to the parents, before the parents die. It should ensure children are not stripped of property, since it does not challenge the status quo of anyone, per se, unlike presenting a will for the first time to people who expect to be beneficiaries. Later in this commentary, Beatrice Were, who is a founder of The Memory Book Project, describes how her memory book liberated her and made her accountable to her children.

Police intervention in recovery of grabbed property

The Victim Support Unit (VSU) was formed in 1994 through the Police Reform Programme. Its headquarters are in Lusaka, Zambia, but the intention is to extend it to other centres. The VSU's objective is to focus on gender violence by prosecuting perpetrators and creating awareness. The existing Intestate Succession Act 1989 has provisions for the division of inheritance: widows are given 20 per cent, parents 20 per cent, other dependents 10 per cent, and children 50 per cent. These amounts vary if, for example, there are no other dependents or the parents are deceased. Property-grabbing is a major problem in Zambia but, through the VSU, the police are empowered to recover property and make arrests. Remaining problems include the reluctance of widows to go to the police and lack of information about succession laws and the VSU. Also, services are too far away for women living in rural areas. Furthermore, widows are often unwilling to press charges, despite the legitimacy of their complaint, often because they are subjected to threats and intimidation or because they do not want to risk breaking family ties. The VSU provides community sensitisation, arrests perpetrators, targets traditional leaders, creates radio and television programmes, networks with other organisations, creates brochures and posters, and has sponsored music concerts that include sensitisation during breaks in performances. Conviction rates have been slowly increasing since the VSU began operating. In 2003, 734 cases of property-grabbing were reported, which, nonetheless, represents only the tip of the iceberg.

Transforming home-based care groups into business groups

GROOTS Kenya is a grassroots NGO working in Nairobi. They have trained 120 home-based volunteers to care for HIV and AIDS patients in Mathare slum in Nairobi. Sadly, of these 120, only 20 have remained committed to continue their work as voluntary carers. They visit their HIV and AIDS sick patients, take water and food to them, wash them, clean their shelter, and cook for them when they find that patients have not been cleaned or have not eaten, sometimes for three days. The carers come home late in the evening, often to find their own children have gone to bed without supper. The carers are also slum dwellers, struggling every day to make ends meet. The members of the home-based care group came up with the idea of setting up a kind of 'shareholding company' for an agro-processing project. Other home-based care groups in Limuru and Kitui also generated business ideas. Three workshops were organised to get these home-based care groups together to meet, discuss, and consolidate their ideas into a proposal. A unique aspect of the project is that it will benefit the children of the home-based care group members who will become shareholders when they are orphaned, as many of the carers are also HIV-positive.

Swazi Positive Living's agricultural co-operatives

Swazis Positive Living (SWAPOL) was founded as a support group to benefit HIV-positive women who shared the problem of stigma. SWAPOL initiated a project involving agricultural co-operatives to support this group. They have training programmes for caregivers, supply medical help to children with HIV and AIDS, offer assistance to abused children and widows, provide home-based care and neighbourhood care points for orphans and vulnerable children (OVC). One means of supporting themselves, and raising funds for OVC, involved SWAPOL approaching chiefs and asking for a field for farming. Their request was granted. Part of their agricultural produce is used for OVC feeding programmes at neighbourhood care points. The income from the sale of products is partly re-invested; the rest being shared between members and spent to assist people living with HIV and AIDS.

The Village of Hope in Rwanda

The Village of Hope was established by the Rwandan Women's Network to accommodate the survivors of the 1994 genocide who were victims of sexual and gender-based violence committed during that time. Today, 100 women, youths and children live in the village and 1 200 people participate in various village-based activities, including income-generating schemes, human rights education, and health and psychosocial support. It is a centre for healing from trauma and encouraging reconciliation. A project on building low-cost housing has provided many widows and children with shelter and a space to start a new life. New plans for the organisation include the acquisition of plots for collective farming, and advocacy on women's land and property rights in the context of HIV and AIDS. Livelihood supports and income-generating activities are considered to be a key to improving the social status of women.

'Reclaiming our lives': Narratives and responses

Pelagia Katunzi, a woman living with HIV from Tanzania, once asked: 'When a woman has lost her husband and a piece of land, where does she get food to feed her children?' Part of the answer is: 'Property and a piece of land give women and children livelihoods and peace of mind', which was the catch phrase for a National Workshop on 'HIV and AIDS, Women's Property Rights and Livelihoods in Zimbabwe', held in Zimbabwe, December 2004. The question remains, however, 'Why do people grab property?' Is it greed, poverty, the exercise of power or the satisfaction which comes from controlling another's life? Indeed, many of the property-grabbers are not poorer but better-off relatives. What drives people to grab a tiny hut, a small piece of land or a cooking pot from a poor widow or orphan, leaving them destitute? Unless this question is answered, we are far from stopping property-grabbing.

It is hoped that this book will support the existing initiatives and will facilitate concrete action to be taken to prevent land and property disputes and to strengthen women's land and property rights in the context of HIV and AIDS. It is our hope that HIV-positive mothers may live even one day longer to look after their children, despite their HIV-positive status, and that widows may live with peace of mind after the death of their husband. We would also like to witness orphaned children living under careful supervision in properties left by their parents and retaining pleasant memories of their parents. It is hoped that the stories related in this book will deepen the understanding of the problem of land- and property-grabbing but with appreciation of the resilience of survivors of property-grabbing and their support groups. It is hoped that small but valuable initiatives by our women and their support groups will inspire other women and organisations who are facing similar situations.

The narratives come from nine countries in southern and East Africa and are grouped by country (in alphabetical order), as that provides the larger context in which the stories unfold. There are two broad categories of narratives – first, stories of HIV-affected women and their children, in which the women recount their personal experiences of property disputes, poverty and the struggles they have waged to reclaim their lives, and second, accounts by women who have been involved in setting up community-based support groups and other types of organisations in response to the HIV and AIDS crisis.

The number of narratives per country is not consistent and there are no claims that the selection of stories presented here is representative of all the issues and types of community-based organisation found in each of these countries or in the region. Rather, the narratives illustrate important dimensions of the crisis and its impact specifically on women and their property rights across the region; at the same time, they also highlight the often heroic, yet unpublicised, ways in which many grassroots organisations are responding to the challenges of the pandemic. The stories and organisations presented in this publication reflect the network that has emerged around FAO's work on these issues in this region over the past few years, and the willingness of individual contributors to participate in this endeavour. All those whose testimonies are included have given their consent to being quoted. We used false names when asked to do so, and endnotes indicate when this occurs.

The interviews were undertaken by Kaori Izumi and members of partner organisations and support groups. Some of the pieces were not from interviews but written by individuals, and others were presentations made at various workshops organised by FAO.

Country profile **Eritrea**

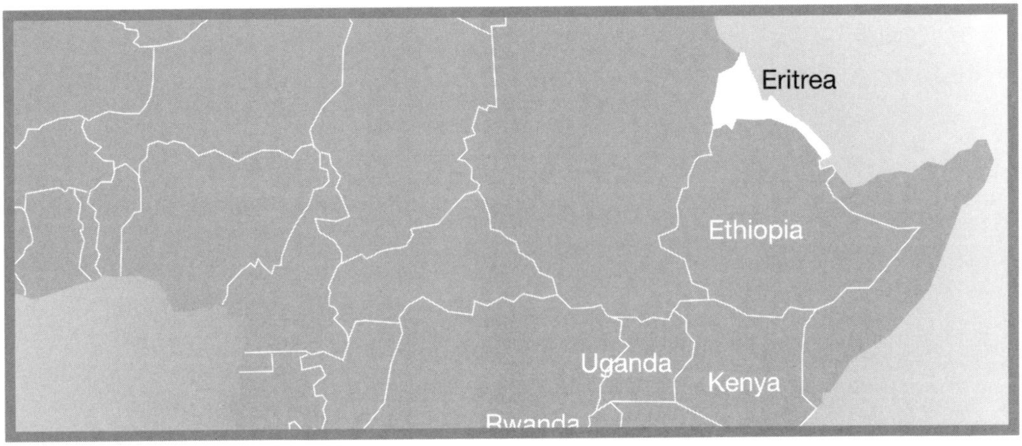

Eritrea is a country with a total population of 4.1 million people. Adult illiteracy rate is as high as 43.3 per cent. The country is classified as one of the few Low-Income Food Deficit Countries (LIFDC) of the world with a GDP per capita of US$171 in 2003 (UNDP 2005). About seven out of ten people are living below the minimum standard of living threshold. In 2000, over 80 per cent of the total population lived in rural areas.

Poverty and food insecurity remain widespread and are growing in Eritrea, accentuated by the effects of severe recurring drought. Eritrea's food insecurity problems have also emanated from the lingering effects of the border conflict with Ethiopia. The war caused immense social and economic damage, including displacement/dislocation and loss of productive assets. Large areas of fertile grounds in the vicinity of the border have been made inaccessible for farming and grazing, due to insecurity and landmines.

Women-headed households represent approximately 30 per cent of households in Eritrea, a legacy of the war of independence and recent conflict. About 70 per cent of the population relies on agriculture, pastoralism or fishing for income and employment. Women represent 50 per cent of the agricultural labour force.

In Eritrea, 60 000 adults and children are living with HIV and AIDS (UNAIDS 2004). Out of 55 000 adults who are living with HIV, 21 000 are women, and there are 5 600 children living with the disease. By 2003, 6 300 people had died of AIDS, creating, as a result, 39 000 orphans.

The Proclamation Act of 1994 declared all land to be the property of the state, abolishing customary land tenure and replacing it with a state-designed system of community–based tenure (Subramanian 1996). The system is viewed as egalitarian and vastly improves the conditions of access to land for many of the previously disadvantaged groups of people, especially women and pastoral populations. Article 15 of the Act, relating to married persons, provides women with equal rights for obtaining usufruct rights over farming land. Article 16 provides divorced spouses with the rights to retain his/her individual usufruct rights over land allotted in accordance with the statute. In the event of a divorced wife returning to her home village, she can obtain land for farming by applying to the Land Administrative Body.

The Family Law of the State of Eritrea co-exists with customary and Sharia laws (Islamic laws) to protect women's rights. Statutory law accords women equal status to men, including in relation to land and property rights. Furthermore, the legislation prohibits any discriminatory action when property is shared, following divorce or death, by providing the wife with half of the marital property, irrespective of whether she contributed financially to its acquisition or not. However, this does not apply to Muslim women, who are governed by Sharia law. This law dictates that females are to receive only a percentage of what their male counterparts receive (Tsehainesh 1998). Thus, a large segment of the female population is denied inheritance rights in Eritrea. Although, at policy level, women are afforded equal land rights, in practice it must be noted that this is not necessarily the case (Zerai 2001).

The bonanza is over

HIV and AIDS, stigma and poverty

KIDAN FELOMON[4]

Interview in Asmara, March 2004 by Worku Zerai, a social development consultant specialising in gender issues

My name is Kidan Felomon. I am a 47-year-old widow and I live in Asmara, the capital of Eritrea. I have nine children. The oldest is 20 and the youngest is 7. My husband died of AIDS in 1999. He was a well-to-do merchant who travelled between Eritrea and Ethiopia. He did not tell me that he was infected with AIDS. Three years before his death I asked the doctor who was looking after him to tell me the cause of his sickness and he told me that my husband was suffering from liver cancer. But later, one of the nurses who were coming to my house weekly told me that my husband was infected with the virus. When I heard that, I was shocked and cried until my husband died. When I found out that I was HIV-positive too, I felt like killing my children and myself, but the nurse helped me to accept the problem and to look after my children.

I told my eldest son and daughter that I was HIV-positive. At first it was so difficult for the children to accept it. They cried for three days and nights. But slowly they started to support me. My daughter undertakes all activities that involve sharp instruments and I do everything that is done with water, like washing clothes, cleaning the house, etc. The eldest boy undertakes income-generating activities. I sometimes participate in the informal business, such as selling vegetables, soap, and matches. But, despite our efforts, our family is underfed. Recently, we started receiving food aid from the government.

The illness of my husband totally impoverished our family. I sold all our furniture and jewellry to support my family and pay for my husband's medical expenses. I had 70–80 g of gold, which my husband had bought for me, but I had to sell that, too. There were times when I could not give food to my children. Once, my children went without food for the whole day. In the evening I gave the last plate of pasta to my husband and did not know what to give to the children. I was going in and out of the house the whole evening, until finally a neighbour realised my situation and left me five pieces of bread, which I divided among my children. The eldest shared his piece of bread with me and then we all went to sleep.

I am a member of an association of people living with HIV and AIDS. But I am not an active member, because many of the members are commercial sex workers and I do not want to be associated with them. I thus fail to get the benefits that I could get from the association.

Before my husband got sick, people used to come to our house and spend the night with us and enjoy the bonanza we used to have. But after he became ill, people started refraining from coming to our house. One day, my husband vomited and asked his mother to help him. Instead of helping him, however, his mother called me, because she was afraid of getting infected. Then my husband told his mother to leave the house for good. She went back to her natal village.

'The illness of my husband totally impoverished our family.'

I have some friends who have similar problems. Among them is a woman whose husband died in 1998. The family depends on farming for a living. They had a plot of land on which they used to plant barley, maize and potatoes. As she could not plough her land, she used to give her land to sharecroppers who were ploughing the land for her. She was responsible for weeding and harvesting. The share-croppers used to give her half of the produce but later, as she became weak, she could not weed, so the sharecroppers gave her only a quarter of the produce and, since this could not support her, she decided not to have her land ploughed and she now depends on food aid. In Eritrea, women do not plough land. Traditionally, ploughing is a male task and ploughing for women is an unacceptable task that has a stigma attached to it.[5]

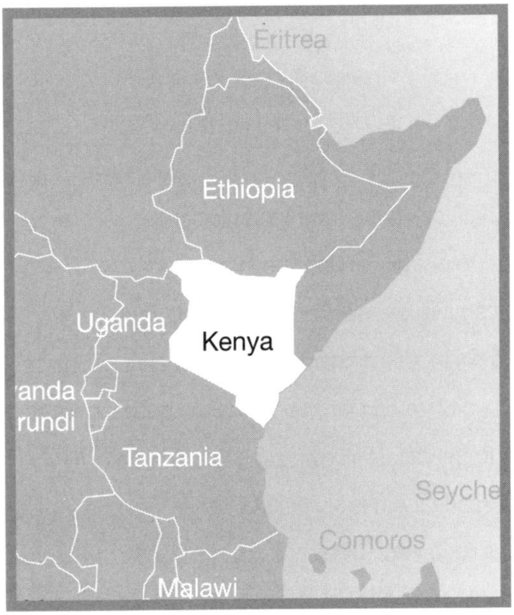

Country profile Kenya

Kenya has a population of 32.7 million people (UNDP 2005). The agricultural sector continues to dominate Kenya's economy, accounting for 24 per cent of the GDP. The sector provides employment for 53 per cent of the labour force and generates over 60 per cent of the value of exports, mainly tea and coffee, but increasingly horticultural products. There is growing competition for land use between farming, pastoral societies grazing and wildlife-based tourism (FAO 2003a). The incidence of malnutrition and poverty is, paradoxically, most serious in the areas of high and medium agricultural potential, where the population density is such that families are only able to farm small plots of land. Kenyan society is characterised by wide income disparities and about half of the population live in poverty.

Around 700 people die daily in Kenya from HIV and AIDS. The pandemic has been declared a national disaster and accounts for the majority of in-patients in the country's hospitals (FAO 2003a). In total 1.2 million people were estimated to be living with HIV, a figure that includes 100 000 children and 720 000 adult women (UNDP 2001).[6] By 2003, 150 000 people had died of AIDS, and 650 000 children had become orphaned as a result of the disease's deadly effects.

Land is divided into private land, un-alienated state land and trust lands, with about 75 per cent devoted to small-scale agriculture under a mix of privatised individual and customary tenure systems. Since the mid 1950s, Kenya has embarked upon a policy of land titling, which has delivered ambiguous results in terms of rural economic development. About 3.2 million hectares have been subdivided into more than 3.5 million holdings with an average ownership of 1.2 hectares (FAO 2003a). Kenya is currently in the midst of a major review of its land policies.

The introduction of private ownership of land in 1986 resulted in the subdivision and registration of individual titles. Land titling is perceived to have eroded women's land rights, although a small minority of women have been able to secure land titles. The Married Women's Property Act recognises women's equal rights to property, and the courts have even applied this law in cases where customary or Islamic law would appear to take precedence. A large majority of women are, however, unaware of these implicit rights, based on a 19th century English law. For testate succession, a woman, whether married or unmarried, has the same capacity to make a will as a man. The limitation is that most family property is registered in the husband's name only. For intestate succession, where one has left a surviving spouse and children, the spouse is entitled to inherit the personal and household effects of the deceased and life interest of the net intestate estate. In the case of a surviving widow, the interest will terminate upon remarriage.

The new Constitution Bill, which was presented on 23 August 2005, allowed women to own land and property and widows to inherit land from their husbands despite the absence of a will. The Bill says, 'A surviving spouse shall not be deprived of a reasonable provision out of the estate of a deceased spouse whether or not the spouse died having made a will' (Ikdahl et al. 2005).

Grassroots Organisations Together in Sisterhood (GROOTS Kenya)

GROOTS Kenya is a network of grassroots women's self-help groups and community organisations that reaches across ethnic and regional boundaries in Kenya. The network was founded immediately after the 4th UN Conference on Women held in Beijing, China, in 1995. It is affiliated to GROOTS International and the Huairou Commission and the Huairou Commission – both members of the International NGO Network, which works with grassroots women's organisations.

The aim of the organisation is to invest in capacity building among poor and vulnerable women, their families and communities, so that they can participate directly in decision-making that affects them and thereby improve their lives. Many poor women are disinherited of their land and property because they have neither strong social-safety networks, nor information about their rights, nor the resources to help them pursue justice.

The activities of the organisation include: home-based care, child-care centres, orphan support, income-generating activities for women, and support groups for people living with HIV and AIDS.

Investing in grassroots women

ESTHER MWAURU-MUIRU
Organiser, GROOTS Kenya
Interview by Kaori Izumi, Mathare, January 2005

The upsurge of HIV and AIDS in Kenya, particularly among illiterate, semi-literate and poor women, has further complicated the existing insecurity surrounding women's land and property rights in Kenya. There are many widows who have lost their matrimonial property rights after their spouses passed away. The worst aggressors are their in-laws, particularly their husbands' brothers. Instead of helping their sister-in-law, many of them grab their property. As more families are stripped of their property and chased out from their rural land, the population of the slums is ever-increasing to accommodate these people. As caring social networks providing the key to ensuring the ability of women in this situation to begin life afresh, while also catering for the needs of their children, we are engaged in programmes on governance, HIV and AIDS and income-generation.

'Women, without any proof, are accused of bringing HIV and AIDS to the family.'

In 2001, we had a mother, Nyambura who was bedridden with AIDS. Her neighbour slowly encroached upon her plot in Korogocho slum. A group of women from GROOTS Kenya in Mathare

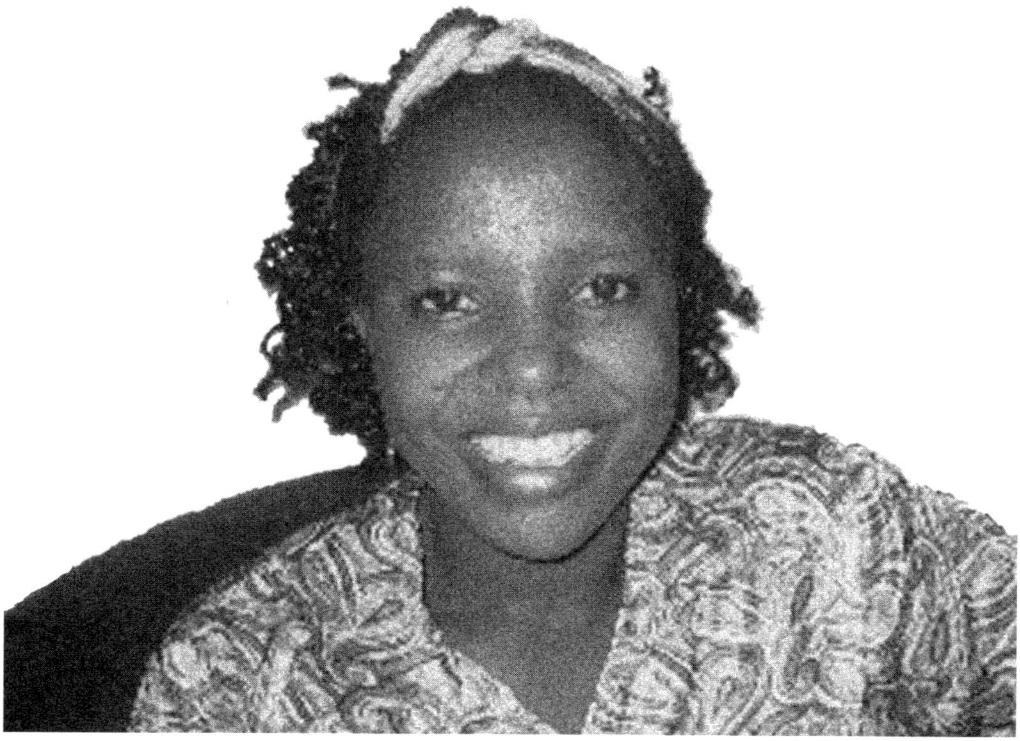

slum travelled to Korogocho and petitioned the chief and finally managed to stop the encroachment. When the mother died, the GROOTS Kenya women tried very hard to secure the piece of land so that her 12-year-old daughter could use it when she grew up. This did not work, as the only document they could find in their house was an allotment letter and not a title deed. The young girl eventually left to live with her grandparents in the rural area. Later on, the women's group decided to find out if Nyambura's daughter was fine and they were happy to learn that her grandparents had gracefully accepted her as part of the family.

Group-therapy sessions for widows and women living positively with HIV and AIDS are also an important component of our programme. In these sessions, women share their problems, which often are similar, and learn survival tactics and coping mechanisms from each other. We are convinced that supporting these groups is an effective investment. Women living with HIV and AIDS have proved to be excellent homecare givers. Our home-based carers provide medical extension services, but the women themselves also benefit through gaining a sense of identity as individuals facing similar challenges.

Many women linked to our organisation are not directly affected by HIV and AIDS, but have also been denied their rights to secure land and property. This presents them with great challenges, including the search for shelter in the slums, and illustrates the importance of addressing the issue of women's insecure land and property rights as a general problem.

I grew up in a small village which was 30 km away from Nairobi. When I was 9 years old, I had to buy food to put on the table at home. It gave me a sense of how to work. I went to a Catholic Missionary School, where I appreciated being involved in support activities in communities. When I joined the university, I had a clear idea on what I wanted to do in my life. I chose sociology and community work. I met people from GROOTS International at the Beijing Conference in 1995. In the tent of women, 100 women met every day, including grassroots women. Grassroots International was established during the 3rd International Women's Conference held in Nairobi in 1985. I established GROOTS Kenya in 1995, immediately after I came back from Beijing. I started mobilising women in Mathare slum.

Women, without any proof, are accused of bringing HIV and AIDS to the family. People threaten women so disproportionately. Kenyan women are tailored to carry the family. At five in the afternoon, after coming back from school, girls are working, fetching water, cooking, etc. Girls are taken out of school. The first to be called to take care of sick people in the family is the wife, mother, daughter or aunt. When we started Mathere Home-Based Care programme, women often did not come to group meetings. We wondered how they could help themselves. Women feared being infected when they cared for their sick family members. HIV and AIDS became the third burden for women. Women have a burden as a person of reproduction, often without choice. Women are producers, and now women have become carers of the HIV and AIDS sick.

There are many women who live in Mathare, not because they were born or married in Mathare, but because they were chased away from their rural homes where they were married. I was surprised to find out that there were many women in Mathare who came there because they were chased out, for various reasons, because their husband had died of HIV and AIDS. In the past, widows were not chased away from marital homes. They were considered as people who needed support to sustain their livelihoods. But since the HIV and AIDS pandemic hit our communities, widows are considered as people who are dying, therefore not needing support. They are also seen as people who brought HIV and AIDS home. People do not want to be seen associating with somebody with HIV and AIDS in the home compound. HIV and AIDS escalated the eviction of widows.

In Africa, especially in my Kikuyu tribe, the dead were respected, which was further enhanced by a Christian influence. When a family had a feast, the family shared food with the dead. With HIV and AIDS, if a person dies of HIV and AIDS, the family wants to forget the person. People do not care. Bitterness over getting HIV and AIDS affects the way in which widows and orphans are treated with hatred. For the same reason, girls are sent away from home and abandoned by their own parents. The sexual part of the cause of the disease makes HIV and AIDS different from other diseases. Most women are affected because their husbands had an extra-marital relationship. HIV and AIDS are usually brought about through cheating relationships. The majority of women affected are married women. In 2004, our home-based care group in Limuru lost seven patients, and Mathare group lost four of their group members.

In the long term, we need a comprehensive policy to protect widows' and orphans' property rights in the context of HIV and AIDS. In the short term, there is a need to provide people with livelihoods so that they can start surviving.

Our challenge is how to make donors understand that work with the community is an intense and long process. It takes a long process to show the outcome of the investment in community works. Transferring the capacity into communities takes a long time. Many donors have difficulty in understanding this fact. Grassroots Kenya decided not to have professional staff members as such, instead we tried to involve community-based women to build their capacity to take a lead and play a central role. My message to donors and our partners is 'start valuing the capacity which a community has and add value to it'. Competition within the donor community undermines linkages and networking among them.

Group therapies of widows and women living positively with HIV and AIDS have played a major role in psychosocial therapy. Women share their problems, which often are similar, and learn tactics and coping mechanisms. GROOTS Kenya is convinced of the effectiveness of investment in these support groups. The women have put savings together in the hope of buying themselves pieces of land. They are also running collective income-generating activities as well as vocational courses for young girls orphaned by HIV and AIDS.

Home-based carer in Mathare

ANN WANJIRU
Member, Mathare Home-based Care Group
Interview by Kaori Izumi, Mathare, September 2003

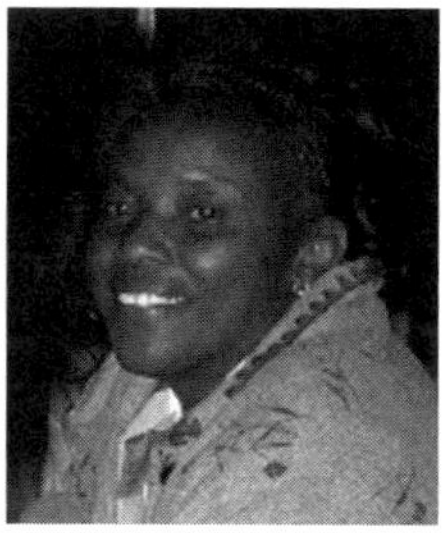

I am a focal point for GROOTS Kenya Mathare Home-based HIV and AIDS Care Group. I am a tailor by profession. I am married and have three children and look after one orphan of my late sister who died of AIDS. I have lost three of my family members to HIV and AIDS. I am one of the 23 people who continue to work as carers out of a total 120 who have been trained by GROOTS Kenya. Around 100 of those who were initially trained dropped out. The carers are supposed to work three days a week for limited hours, but we often end up working longer hours as we find our patients without having eaten for three days and without any water. Carers look for money to buy water and food; often we use our money, which we should spend to buy water and food for our own family. Sometimes I work caring for my patients until late in the evening and come home only to find my children gone to bed without supper.

When I visit my patients, I can never visit them empty-handed because I know they have not eaten. I always have to carry some food. If there is money from group savings, I use that money, and if not, I still need to buy food with my own money. Sometimes I do not visit my patients when I have nothing to bring to them. Many of my patients ask me for help for school fees, complaining that their children were chased away from school as they had failed to pay school fees. My children have also been out of school several times when I was not able to pay school fees, but my patients simply do not know that I have the same problem. Our work is not sustainable as all the carers are totally worn out and more members are becoming seriously sick, becoming bedridden. We have lost some of our carers, many of whom are also HIV-positive. It is a traumatic experience each time your patient dies. We meet at our Mathare Mothers' Centre to counsel each other, giving each other psychosocial support. Many of the carers dropped out because of the trauma they had to go through. Why I am doing this? I do not know, perhaps one day God will help me because I am helping others.

From home-based care into business

An entrepreneurial approach to HIV and AIDS home-based care-giving

LUCY MUGUIYI NJUGUNA

Consultant

This article was written in March 2005 to describe a joint initiative taken by GROOTS Kenya and FAO to support home-based care groups.

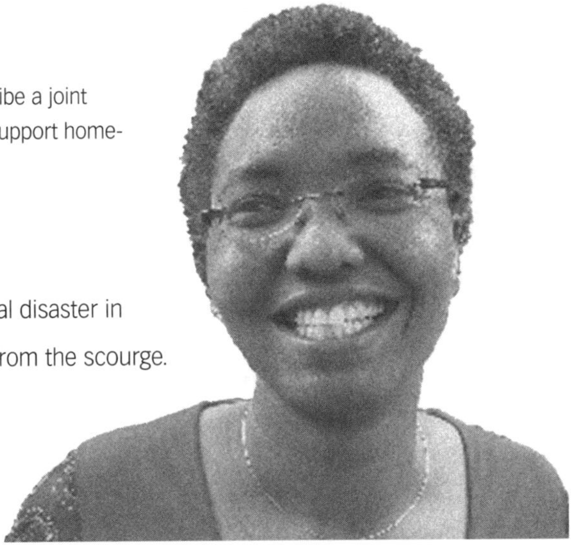

HIV and AIDS have been declared a national disaster in Kenya. Thousands of lives have been lost from the scourge. As home managers, women have disproportionately shouldered the task of nursing and feeding the sick family members. To support their efforts, GROOTS Kenya has been conducting capacity-building workshops for training of trainers on HIV and AIDS home-based care. However, despite the commitment, the weak resource base has become a hindrance to their effectiveness in serving the community as caregivers. Three groups that had embraced the care-giving vision were selected to become part of a pilot project supported by FAO to develop group-owned commercial enterprises that would not only support the participating members, but also provide the medical supplies and nutritional support needed by the infected persons in the selected communities.

Tei Wa W'o self-help group, which means 'true mercy', is located in Kitui District, and is a composite of ten independent sub-groups. The group provides free home-based care to people living with HIV and AIDS (PLWHA). The group is planning to expand its current grain-consolidation centre into a leading cereal-consolidation centre in Eastern Province. The business opportunity that the group seeks to exploit is that of purchasing and consolidating grains cheaply during the harvest season and reselling the grains to the community, particularly when the demand is high, for profit. The group will register a business name for this business. Capacity will be built to make it a company limited by guarantee. The business will be managed by a business committee but the overall business- management capacity needs to be strengthened in order for the group to achieve its objectives.

The second group is Mathare Mothers' Development Centre. The group is located in the heart of Mathare slum and is made up of over 30 self-help groups. The group's focus is to provide free home-based care to PLWHA. The group has been involved in income-generation through its day-care centre. It has plans to expand its business by starting a posho mill that will mill and pack several nutritious flour-product lines for the market to meet the needs of their target clients. The group has developed a comprehensive marketing strategy that will ensure its products reach the target market. This being a slum area, the socio-economic dynamics of the nature of the planned business is more complex.

The third group, Mwihoko Wa Rironi self-help group, is located in Limuru, on the outskirts of Nairobi. Currently, the group has been contributing weekly towards the support of PLWHA and orphans and vulnerable children (OVC). The group is, at present, selling maize as a business, but on a limited scale. The group intends to establish a cereals-consolidation centre and a posho mill that will offer a Mwihoko brand of milled flour. The group will register a business name and later, as their business capacity grows, become registered as a limited company. The overall business leadership will be provided by the group's business executive committee. GROOTS wishes to equip members of these groups with:

- Business-planning skills;
- Entrepreneurial skills;
- Financial-management skills;
- Organisational-development skills.

'A transformed woman transforms the family and, in turn, the nation.'

Furthermore, GROOTS wants to provide linkages, noting that these groups come from different zones and offer different products which can leverage each other's business ventures. Overall, the intervention will create sustainable social-economic support systems for the women and their communities at large and build their capacity to empower themselves for sustainability.

It is exciting to see how this project will develop. Capacity building is a key to its success. Giving these women management and business skills will help them not only make informed decisions on this business venture but in their daily lives, also. A transformed woman transforms the family and, in turn, the nation. This is an exciting place to invest our resources and our lives.

Dreaming of a piece of land

ALICE KAROKI[7]
Member, Mathare Home-based Care Group
Interview by Kaori Izumi, Mathere, January 2005

I was born 33 years ago. In 1989 I was married to a 39-year-old man. We moved to Nairobi, to the Mathare slums where we stayed together. In the sixth year of our marriage, I got my second born baby, this time a girl. During that pregnancy my husband developed different types of ailments and succumbed to death two weeks after I had given birth. I accompanied the body to his rural home for burial, together with my children, some household utilities and furniture. My in-laws were very uncooperative and never allowed any of my relatives to accompany me to the rural areas for burial. My sister opted to take different transport from the burial convoy because she could sense animosity. When we arrived home, I found that the door to our rural house had been removed. When I asked about it, my in-laws told me that it was under repair. I later realised that this was to ensure that my children and I would not live there after my husband was safe in the grave. I was told to take my children away to my family as I had killed their son. I inquired about the piece of land where our house was standing but I was told that my husband had no share of inheritance in that family. Apparently, my husband was the first-born from his mother's womb but was born before she married into this family. I was thus informed that if I needed any inheritance then I should search for my biological father-in-law and claim land there.

Before I left home, I decided to seek the intervention of the assistant chief, who provided guidance for arbitration. It was agreed that I should inherit at least the piece of land that hosted my husband's grave, as well as the house we had constructed together. However, this did not stop my in-laws' ruthlessness. They sold all the items I had brought from Nairobi, without my consent, and shared among themselves the rest. Two months later, the assistant chief was reported murdered and my late husband's relatives were said to be the culprits. I was scared and decided to leave the compound without a clear idea of my destiny. I travelled across the Uganda-Kenya border, where I met one of my sister's families. According to our traditions, if your spouse or child dies, you cannot sleep in another person's house for some months. Therefore, neither my mother nor my sisters, though they loved me dearly, could allow me to sleep in their houses. My sister gave me bus fare to travel back to

Nairobi. I was shocked to find out that my in-laws had travelled secretly to Nairobi, sold all our property and the landlord had already been informed that I no longer needed the house. A friend who is not of my tribe allowed me into her house; she sheltered us for weeks and later gave me money to start up a business. Together with my sister's support, I was able to move to my own house and started off life once again with my children.

In November 1999 I started getting ill and that is when I was diagnosed with HIV. My little daughter, too, was already infected. I was so sick that my mother came for me to Nairobi. When I was bedridden she took me with her to the rural home. I stayed there until January 2001, when I decided to come back to Mathare to make a living for my two children and myself. I was once again shocked that my in-laws had trashed my house and had lied to the landlord that I had died and they had been allowed to fetch all my household effects. The landlord was annoyed, too, and decided to give me the house back, despite the fact that I already had accumulated rent arrears for eight months during my ailment. In February 2001, I met GROOTS Kenya and they assisted me with bedding and a few personal belongings to start my life once more. I am one of the founder members of the GROOTS Kenya support group for people living with HIV. I feel lucky, since I have learnt a lot through the many training courses, exchanges and interactions with other members in Kenya, and their partners. My children, a 13-year-old son and a 6-year-old daughter, are much happier. We dream one day that we can have a piece of land, build ourselves a secure house and forget our struggles. If I die, I would want my children to have secure tenure of land as they have already gone through enough trauma. Fortunately, they are lovely and very mature and provide me with strong companionship and respect.

One day when I get better...

ANNA NDONGE
Member, Mathare Home-based Care Group
Interview by Kaori Izumi, Mathare slum, Nairobi, September 2003

I am 26 years old. I grew up in Mathare. I was married to a man from Machakos, who was a casual labourer in Nairobi. I met him in Nairobi. When he fell seriously ill, I took him to his home in Machakos where he later died in 1997 of HIV and AIDS. After he died, I also fell ill. My mother-in-law did not give me food. I was abandoned in my bed for two weeks without any food and care. I told one of our neighbours, 'I am very sick and I am dying.' The person I talked to sent a message to my mother in Mathare. My mother came and found that I was left without food and any care by my in-laws for two weeks. I moved to Mathare in 1999. We lived in another shack but we were evicted from there as we were not able to pay the rent. The owner of the shack threw our belongings out from our house. When this happened, I was seriously sick with tuberculosis, sitting outside the shack. When the owners were throwing out our belongings, one woman passed by and she offered us her shack as our new home. The woman was an owner of shacks in Mathare and used one of them only when she visited Mathare to collect rents. She told us that we could stay there.

In Mathare, there is a German feeding programme for orphans, the seriously sick and people living with HIV and AIDS. Every Wednesday my mother collects 2 kg of maize and 1 kg of beans for me, which two adults and three children as our family share. In addition, I receive cooked food, rice and beans during weekdays. There is no feeding during weekends. Beneficiaries are only those who are referred by the hospital, but many of us are not able to physically collect food as we are too sick even to walk. Mathare Home-based Care Group helps with collection of food for their clients. We need to buy charcoal to cook maize and beans, which is often a problem as one sack of charcoal costs Ksh.300 (about US$4 in 2003). I feel good when there is heat of charcoal which warms me up. At times I feel better and can walk to GROOTS Kenya's Mothers' Centre. I used to work as a home-based carer for other HIV and AIDS sick patients, together with my mother, but I am not able to do so any longer as my health condition deteriorated during recent months.

When I moved to Mathare, my mother took me to a German clinic, which I was referred to by the Kenyatta National Hospital. We travelled to Kenyatta National Hospital from Mathare, but when we arrived at the hospital we realised that we had to pay for a medical card before I could see a doctor. Even if we had the money for the card, we would not have been able to pay for medicine. We decided to go back home without seeing a doctor, but my mother did not have a single cent with her to take transport back to Mathare. We tried to seek help at the hospital, but nobody could help us. We waited until seven in the evening, and then my mother told me that we had to walk home as our children were waiting for us at home without food. We started walking. When I collapsed on the way, two robbers came to us and searched our bags only to find that there was nothing to take. My mother asked the robbers if they could give us Ksh.20 (50 cents, US) for transport to go back home. The robbers told her that we were lucky that if it was others, we would have been raped. The robbers left us. I somehow managed to stand up to walk again. When we reached home, it was one o'clock in the morning. We walked for six hours from the hospital. We found three cups of flour at home. My mother cooked porridge. I ate one cup, my three children shared the rest, and my mother went to bed with an empty stomach.

'I was abandoned in my bed for two weeks without any food and care.'

If I could get better food, I would be healthier and I could work for our patients again. If I could get better, I will work hard. And one day, I will get a piece of land of my own.

Anna goes on *safari*

JOYCE WAYUA
Member, Mathare Home-based Care Group
Interview by Kaori Izumi, Mathare slum, Nairobi, January 2005

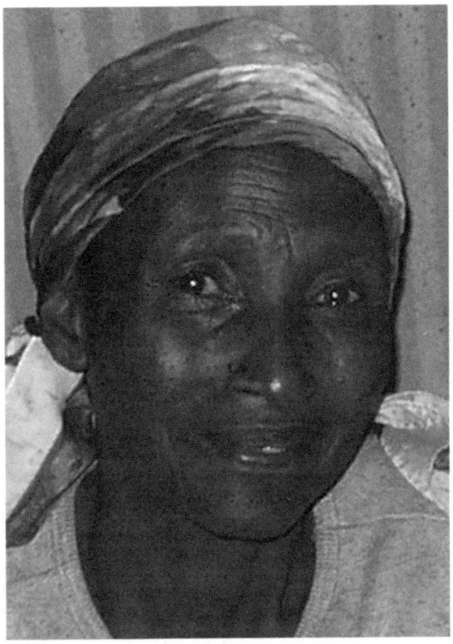

I am a 50-year-old widow from Machakos. I am Anna's mother. I got married in Machakos. My husband was a farmer. His parents were already dead when my husband died and I was chased away by his relatives. My in-laws sold our land and our other family assets. I moved to my brother's home as my parents were dead. Then my husband's relatives came and took away his property equivalent to what my family had received as dowry – five cattle and four goats. They said that it was because when I got married, my husband's family paid dowry to my family. When this happened, my brother was seriously ill. My brother died and the land was too small for his family to share. I left Machakos because of poverty and I moved to Mathare slum to look for a job. I did not know anybody in Mathare. I took jobs like washing clothes and agricultural labour. I became a member of Mathare Home-based Care Group, helping people who were HIV and AIDS sick.

When I got a message that my daughter Anna was seriously ill and dying, it took some days for me to arrange transport, but I managed it finally and arrived in Machakos. When I found Anna in bed, she was too weak to speak. I cooked some food the first day and took her to the nearest hospital. Anna was improving and could speak and walk. I took Anna to Mathare. I carried only two dresses for Anna. The children carried nothing because Anna's mother-in-law refused her to take anything else. The mother-in-law told them that everything in the house belonged to her son, even those two dresses. I took them secretly and hid them. It was in 1998 when there was a heavy rain.

I used to work as an agricultural labourer, but since I had my leg and shoulders hurt, I have no longer been able to work. My family, with my daughter Anna and my three grandchildren, are without any cash income, living on a feeding programme for HIV and AIDS sick. We are also assisted by our neighbours and members of GROOTS Kenya, Mathare Home-based Care Group. Ann, who is a focal point for GROOTS Kenya, Mathare, has been trying to find some income-generating activity for me. As

I have to look after Anna, I cannot go away from home. Ann says that perhaps selling some maize and beans nearby our home could be an option for me through which I could generate some small income. I need Ksh.3000–5000 (US$40–70) as initial capital.

During the last two years, Anna had been very ill, but whenever she was feeling slightly better, she wanted to visit her patients. One month before Anna died, she called all her children to her bed and told them: 'I might go for a *safari*[8], which I will stay for a very long time. If I don't come back, you should all stay with your grandmother, respect her and she will take care of you.'

The eldest daughter, Lucia, started crying, understanding that her mother would die. Before Anna died, she used to say: 'Once I get better, I will work and buy a piece of land so that our children can live happily like other children and go to a good school.'

My daughter Anna died on 13 March 2004. We buried her on 30 March. Before she died, Anna wrote a letter to her children to read when she died. She wrote that she had left the children under the care of Rose, Esther and Kaori.

I was selected as one of the beneficiaries of Mathare 4A slum-upgrading project, funded by Germany. They are building houses, one of which I will be soon moving into with my grandchildren.

Anna had three children: Lucia, now 12 years old, Francis, 10 years old and David, 8 years old.

Lucia: 'My dream is to get a farm, live happily with grandmother, help her, finish school and get a job. I want to be a doctor.'

Francis: 'I want to get into a boarding school. I want to get a farm of our own, build a nice house made of stone, buy household goods, get beds and other furniture, and a big farm where we can cultivate maize, bananas, beans, peas, mangos and pawpaw. We can achieve our dream only by working hard to pass exams. My dream is to become a pilot.'

David: 'My dream is to become a driver.'

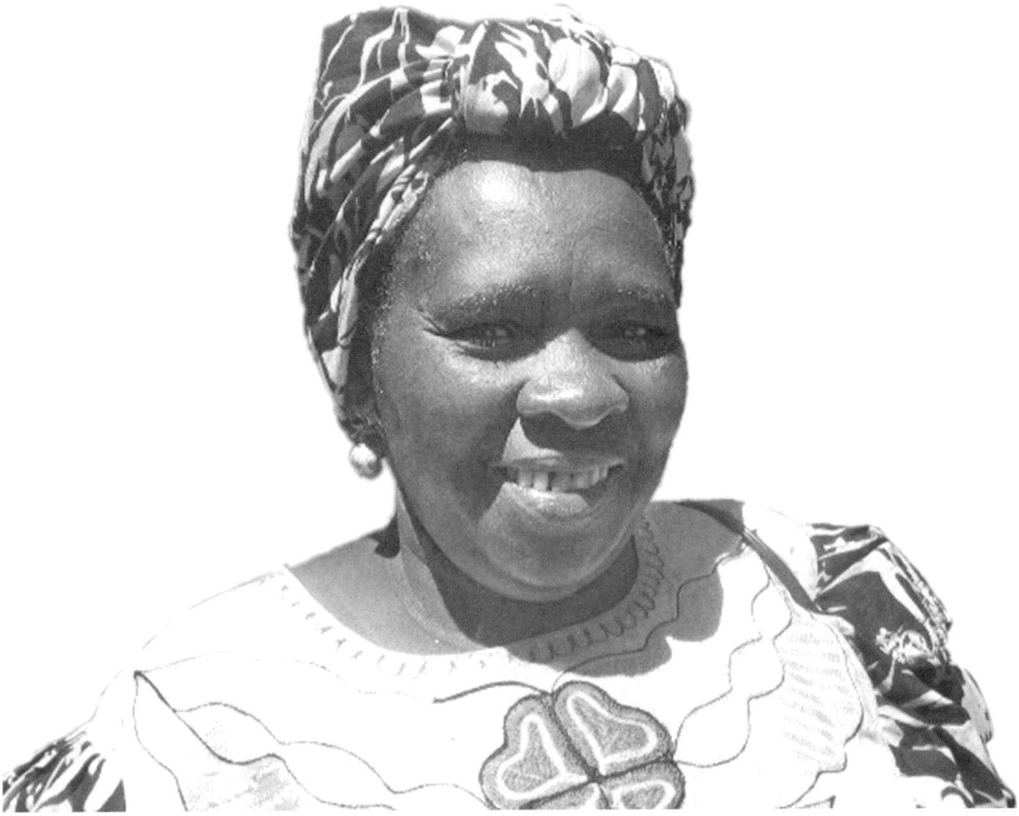

Women video-producers becoming land-owners

MARY NJERI KAMANDE
Member, Slum-dwellers' Association and Mathare Home-based Care Group
Interview by Kaori Izumi, Mathare slum, Nairobi, January 2005

I am a 53-year-old widow. My husband died in 2002. I have seven children and four grandchildren. I live in Redeemed village in Huruma, Nairobi. I have my own house, which I got under 1995 slum upgrading. Since 1978, I have lived in Huruma. I originally come from Muranga district in Central Province. I moved to Nairobi in 1974. My husband was a tailor. I had a problem with my mother-in-law and that was the reason why we moved to Nairobi. We had 1.5 acres of land in the village.

I have been working as a community-work volunteer since 1992. I became a member of Slum-dwellers' Association in 1998. It was under President Moi who had repressive policies for slum-dwellers. Some of us were detained and others killed. We were determined to fight for slum-dwellers' land rights. In 2000, Intermediate Technology Development Group (ITDG) asked me to bring twelve women to participate in a video project. I approached 12 women, but only 9 of them agreed to participate in the project. Others were not interested because it was for free without any payment. Of the 9, only 8 women remained to complete the project.

In 2002, we attended a two-week training, which was organised by ITDG. We were two groups from Mathare slum and were given two video cameras, one for each group. Our neighbours told us that women who were illiterate were doing stupid things. Some of the women who refused to participate in the project because it was for free told us that they would stone us if we came to their area. I told our project members, 'Let's do what we are doing, even if we may be abused!'

After six months, we completed shooting a video. We took all the problems we women in the slum were experiencing. So the video includes, for instance, a scene in which a woman is serving breakfast to her husband first before she goes to her community work; a scene in which a woman and her family are living like goats in a ten-by-ten house; a scene which showed a slum-dweller, who had her house demolished, who was paying a bribe to a chief before the house should be repaired; a scene where a slaughterhouse for goats was built near our house and whatever was coming out from the slaughter was also coming into our house; a village which had only one toilet for 500 people and no service to empty it when it was full. Some were using a 'flying toilet' with a paper bag and throwing it away in the evening. There were so many goats on the road and children were pushed from the street, but a chief did not listen to complaints by parents because the goats belonged to big shots …

'We were determined to fight for slum-dwellers' land rights.'

Our video was shown by Kenyan Television Network (KTN). We were given a Ksh.50 000 (US$700) award from the Barclays Bank. We deposited the money in our group bank account. ITDG sent our video to London and we received Ksh.600 000 (US$8 600) as an award. In 2004, we bought a plot for our group, sub-divided the plot into 3 acres for each of us. We all got individual title on our plot and we paid Ksh.262 606 for eight titles. We donated Ksh.10 000 to Mathare Home-based Care Group and Redeemed Village Home-based Group. The plot is located at Ruai estate outside of Nairobi, 30 minutes travel by commuters. There is no paid work in the area and we have no money to build a house, and there is no water supply. But when I manage to build a house on the plot and move to my new house, I would like to start training women in the area on home-based care so that they can join me to look after their patients.

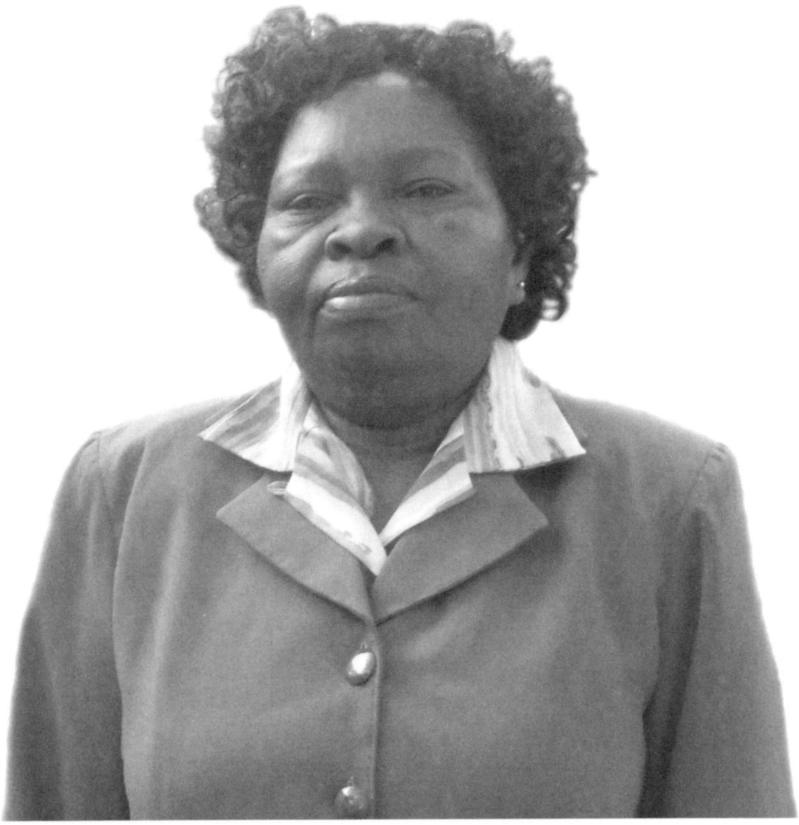

AIDS took my son and my property

BEATRICE WANJIRU MUGUIYI

Interview by her daughter, Lucy Muguiyi Njuguna, Nairobi, January 2005

It was in the morning on Christmas Day 1990. The sky was blue with no clouds to be seen. I had woken up early, as usual, knowing that I had to prepare breakfast before attending Christmas service at our local church nearby. Then I saw him, my first-born and only son. He looked so thin and tired; one shoulder was actually stooping on one side, his right side. He had just woken up, probably intending to go back to bed after answering the call of nature. I felt troubled; I called him. I asked him whether he was feeling all right. He tried to brush it aside, but I felt right in my heart that all was not well. When I asked him whether he had seen a doctor, he said he had seen a much-qualified one, unlike the ones we had near our home in the rural village. I dismissed the issue but my heart was still heavy and troubled.

I remembered the last time I saw him he was healthy and had even developed some muscles, like a person who was eating and living well. He had just completed an Accounting and Administration course in Pakistan, where the bank he worked for had sent him on a short course. He had started working there immediately after graduating with a Bachelor of Commerce degree from the University of Nairobi in 1985.

I had heard and read widely about HIV and AIDS because I like reading. I had read about the symptoms that I could see in my son, but my heart refused to accept the reality. This was the most agonising part of it; I kept everything to myself. How would I talk about this then little-known disease that was associated with evil? Where would I start? How would I explain everything? He went back to work in January but not for long; he was brought home in mid-February, seriously ill. He was in the hospital on and off until 23 May when he passed away in hospital. We buried him a week later on 1 June 1991.

The agony of knowing what he was suffering from, and not talking to anybody, especially the last time he was in hospital, was too much to bear. Mentioning the word 'AIDS' was like a taboo. Even when he was isolated to another ward, as a mother I still wanted to believe that all was normal. Even when we were not allowed to view his body that had grown so small for the last few days, I still just wanted to believe that all was well. It was painful knowing that he was my first child, a boy and the only boy I had. After him, I was blessed with four daughters who are now married with children.

My home district is Nyeri in Central Province. I was lucky to be sent to school at the early age of eight years. This was during the struggle for Kenya's independence. By then girls were not being educated. In fact, I experienced a lot of problems and opposition. My father was also humiliated because of me. Other men would not allow him to participate in their talks or attend parties, but his mind was set. I passed and was admitted to The Alliance Girls High School. I was the first girl to go to high school in the whole district. I became a pioneer.

I joined teaching in 1960. I was excited. I had more money than any woman around! I therefore undertook heavy responsibilities; I sent my two brothers to school in class five and my sister joined class one. My parents were still in the village and I built a house for them where our *shamba*[9] is even now. I planted tea as a cash crop. All this I did in two years. This made the neighbours that had scorned my father about my education start praising him saying, 'Roberti has got a fighting bull', meaning it is only a son who would have managed to do what I had done.

I got married in September 1961. Married life was not easy; being a career woman those days was not easy. A woman was supposed to be in the kitchen or in the garden or feeding children. I was none of those. My husband was ridiculed about this and, unfortunately, he gave in. This is where my trouble started. He started taking advantage of my money; he refused to take the responsibility for feeding, clothing, even sheltering the family, and so I was left to do all these. He even went ahead to bring his relatives, who I also educated. He refused to educate our five children, especially the girls. Life was extremely difficult because the salary was now too stretched. However, I thank God that we never slept hungry, we had clothes and a shelter, and life went on.

After realising that our marriage was headed for the rocks, I started wondering where to get a piece of land to build a family house. This was in 1968. I had moved from Nairobi to the rural area after life in town became too expensive. I decided to settle in a rural area, as the lifestyle was cheaper. I bought some land and by the end of 1968 I had built a new wood-and-tin-roof house.

Developing this *shamba* was an enormous challenge, and this is the fate of most career women. I still had my teaching job, I was single-handedly looking after a big and young family, and I was sitting for exams as a private candidate to enhance my education. I passed and was promoted. After three years I read again privately, then attempted and passed the Advanced National exams and was promoted again. My efforts were paying dividends and my salary kept increasing all this time. I had been teaching in primary school, but after four years, in 1979, I was called to head a girls' secondary school in the district. It is now a big school and I am proud to have been its first Headmistress.

In the midst of this success, little did I know that my promotion was going to affect my marriage to such an extent. My husband was clearly not amused. However, much though I tried to submit and bring the family together, he kept talking ill of 'educated women'. I decided to concentrate on my children's education, teaching and administration. Many were the days that I felt sick, tired and stressed, but I had no alternative but to move on. The reality was I was married, yet I was a single mother. My girls can testify that when we realised that the whole responsibility of bringing up children was mine, I became very strict with their discipline. I was a no-nonsense mother. I thank God that they all later got saved, a factor that helped them to move in life successfully.

After my son died, I experienced a lot of pain but that was not all. As we normally say, death is an enemy. I didn't know until then that my husband had given up on our family and that he was intending to get married to an 'agreeable' wife. He had come to believe that he was rich, but had no heir since our son had died. To quote him, he said, 'I have no heir, only five prostitutes,' meaning four daughters and their mother. I was deeply hurt, but sorry for him as he didn't realise that there was no difference between boys and girls these days. He went and 'married' an illiterate woman who had four sons and two daughters who were all grown, and none belonged to him. I was told to leave our home with only the clothes I was wearing. The grown children who invaded my home for some reason are hostile and it is practically impossible even to go and tend my son's grave, a fact that is emotionally devastating. For me, therefore, the death of my son was a double tragedy in that it also heralded the loss of the home I loved.

I was still heading a school and did not want any confrontation. I discussed the issue with the girls and their husbands. We all decided to choose the way of peace to let him have his way. After all, he was the head of the family. What was most shocking for me and my girls was when we realised that his relatives were on his side! We no longer belonged. We were outcasts! Was this all because of the issue of an heir? The question still troubles my mind.

You may now ask – how do I live? Where? I struggled to raise children. Our son died of AIDS. It affected all of us and my marriage. I struggled to buy and develop our *shamba* and I don't live there any more as my husband lives there with his second family. Do I have any property rights over my grabbed land?

I filed a court case to reclaim my property in the High Court of Nairobi in 1999 – to date the case is dragging in court. Justice is still far off. Delaying tactics are employed left and right, and justice delayed is justice denied.[10]

Six months later

On 8 July, 2005, I felt an inner urge to visit my first home. I was more convinced than ever that I had the right to my house and land. I sought the help of community leaders and peacefully walked into my home. I made it clear to my husband that the home was rightfully mine and I had come back. The reaction was nothing less than a miracle. Without any fight they packed and left. There was great rejoicing as, where the courts failed, it's only courage and an understanding of my rights that won the day. Now I am busy rebuilding my life; ten years are lost, but my joy is complete. This is truly the hand of God.

Country profile **Rwanda**

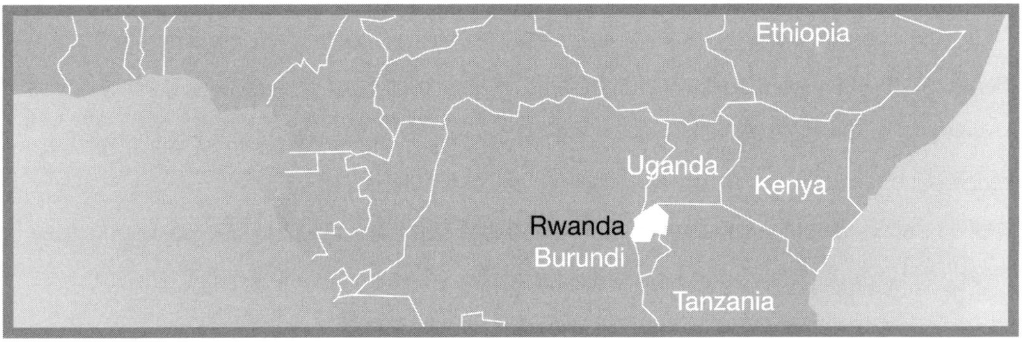

Rwanda, located in the mountainous and hilly areas of Central Africa, has a population of around 8.8 million people (UNDP 2005). The GDP per capita is US$195. Rwanda is the least urbanised country in central Africa. Agriculture accounts for 41 per cent of the GDP. Rwanda's economy is based on the largely rain-fed agricultural production of small, semi-subsistence and increasingly fragmented farms (US State Department 2005).

In 2003, 250 000 adults and children were estimated to be living with HIV, including 130 000 adult women and 22 000 children. By 2003, 22 000 had died of AIDS and 160 000 children were orphaned as a result. The HIV prevalence in young pregnant women in the capital city was estimated to be 11.6 per cent in 2002.

The country has a long history of violent conflict, which has created a huge refugee problem in the neighbouring countries of Uganda, Tanzania and the Democratic Republic of Congo. About 90 per cent of the population practise agriculture. Land is divided into state lands, community-based tenure systems and rights to land that are supported through written law and are dependent upon the registration of land with the state. Land scarcity is high; hence cultivation has encroached into wetlands, national parks and forest reserves. Rwanda is the most densely populated country in sub-Saharan Africa. In average terms, the size of family holdings declined from 3 hectares per family in 1949 to 0.7 hectares by the early 1990s. Rwanda's Land Policy was approved by Cabinet in February 2004 (OXFAM GB 2004).

Rwandan customary law provides for paternal succession where land and housing transfer passes from the father to son (COHRE 2004). Further, any property held by a female has to pass to her son(s) upon her death. A married woman has no ownership rights and effectively is not allowed to receive any property from her husband. The household assets, primarily land and housing, are always considered to be the property of the husband and his lineage. The harassment of widows is commonplace in post-conflict Rwanda. In-laws and other community members regularly divest widows of their homes (COHRE 2004). In 1999, the parliament of Rwanda passed the Inheritance and Succession Law. This new law implicitly grants equal rights to male and female children, establishes a choice of property regimes upon marriage, and allows a wife to inherit her deceased husband's property. This law has greatly enhanced property rights for married women. However, a major drawback is that it only protects monogamous civil marriages. Polygamous marriages are not recognised by civil law and thus do not fall under the protection of the legislation.

A further problem with the Succession Law is that it does not address the inheritance of land, but only refers to housing and personal property. Rwanda is in the process of drafting a policy which, hopefully, will redress this very critical omission. The new policy is also expected to settle the legacy of land disputes.

The Rwanda Women's Network (RWN)

The RWN is a national non-governmental organisation working in Rwanda since 1997. It took over from its parent organisation, the Church World Service, which had a mandate for a two-year programme that started in 1995. The RWN was established with the mission of working towards the promotion and improvement of the socio-economic welfare of women in Rwanda, through enhancing their efforts to meet their basic needs. The organisation's objectives include:

- Empowering poor women and widows economically in the rural and urban areas;
- Fostering economic and social growth within households and communities;
- Improving the health status of widows and orphans;
- Promoting peace and reconciliation.

The RWN implements four core programmes. These include provision of health care and health support, education and awareness programmes on different issues affecting women, including HIV and AIDS, human/legal rights, sexual gender-based violence, and socio-economic empowerment, as well as networking and advocacy. One such initiative, the Polyclinic of Hope, is a project to assist victims of rape and violent crimes.

Women networking for peace

MARY BALIKUNGERI
Executive Director, RWN
Interview by Kaori Izumi, March 2005

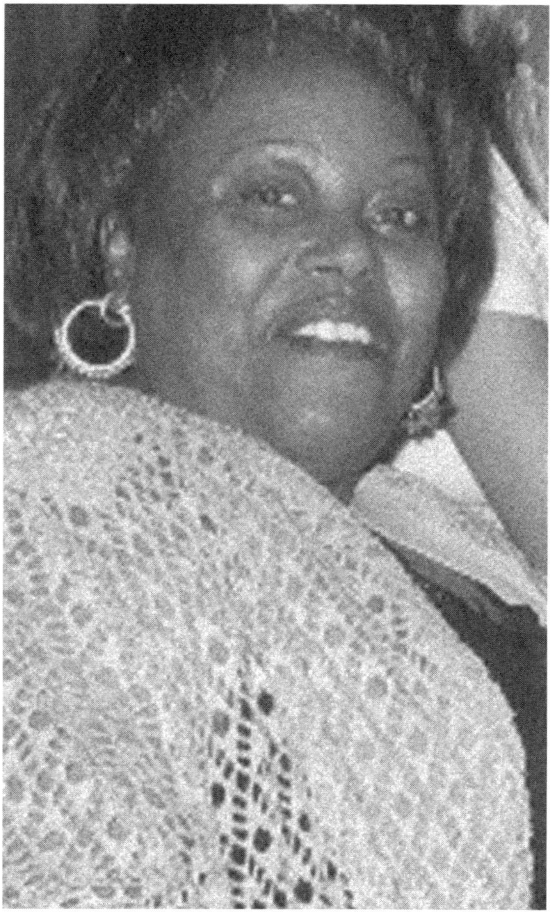

The RWN was established in 1995, following the genocide of 1994. Its objective then was to support widows and orphans who survived the disaster. One of the most critical issues at that time was how to support orphans of the genocide. We set up a fostering programme, identifying fostering families for orphans and supporting the families with economic activities. During the conflict, half the Rwandan population crossed borders to seek refuge in neighbouring countries, which left many houses abandoned. Widows occupied these empty houses. When the government started to stabilise the post-genocide situation, they wanted to return the houses to their rightful owners. Then widows were objecting, 'They killed my family and now I am told to leave.'

We started a low-cost housing project for widows to respond to this situation. We have constructed about 200 low-cost houses all over the country, which are now occupied by widows. Women were involved in brick-making. We negotiated with local authorities to allocate a piece of land for our housing project. Every family got a document for a three-year lease agreement with the local authority in the area. We are trying to convert the leasing document into a title deed, starting with the Kigali urban area. Rwanda is a country with a serious land shortage problem and there is little land for farming. We are promoting nutrition gardening for our women. Each woman who was given a house has a small gardening plot around her house, but it is too small. We are planning to negotiate with local authorities to provide us with a collective farming plot. We also supported women to renovate the houses where they used to live with their husbands before the genocide, putting on a door and adding iron sheets.

We have established a 'Village of Hope' in Kigali in order to accommodate the survivors of sexual and gender-based violence from the genocide. The Village of Hope emerged as a community development initiative as a direct result of the women's experiences at the Polyclinic of Hope. The Village provides shelter for the displaced and disinherited women. The construction of shelters and renovation of housing programmes has provided women with important space for healing and peace-building. The Village provides health services through the Polyclinic of Hope. It organises income-generating activities, sensitisation on HIV and AIDS, and education on human and legal rights relating to marriage and inheritance laws. In total, 100 women, youths and children live in the Village today. There are also 1 200 members of the Village of Hope who are involved in various activities at the Village. Our wish is to build more Villages of Hope in Rwanda.

'We have many cases of property-grabbing.'

We have many cases of property-grabbing, some of them related to HIV and AIDS, but no systematic documentation has been made on this issue, and this is an area for our future work. There is a clear linkage between poverty, commercial sex and HIV infection. One of the most important answers to this problem is economic empowerment for women, which will give women social status and security.

We started working in a situation where two women (one a victim of sexual violence and the other the wife of a man who had abducted other women) were washing clothes, standing next to each other. This is where we started our work of reconciling and building peace after the genocide. We have made progress, but there are still a lot of challenges in front of us.

Step by step on the road to recovery

ROSE MUKABALISA[11]
Member, Polyclinic of Hope Centre
Interview by the RWN, March 2005

My name is Mukabalisa. I was born in 1959 in Shyorongi-Rwahi in Kigali, Rural Province. I am a survivor of the 1994 genocide living at the Village of Hope, Kagugu Sector, Gisozi District in Kigali, Urban Province. I am a woman living with HIV and AIDS, with one daughter and five sons. My first husband died in 1987 and I separated from my second husband before the 1994 genocide because of ethnic tensions at that time. He took all the property and cash we had and left me with the children.

After seeing the problems I was going through, a friend of mine (a widow) living in another province gave me one house among three houses she had on a plot in Kigali city. I used to manage her property, collect the rent and then send the money to her. The 1994 genocide took place when I was living in this situation. I was found in this house and gang-raped by Interahamwe militia while my children watched. This went on for about one month until I sought refuge in a nearby church. On the way to the church at night, I was stopped at a road block and beaten.

At the end of the 1994 genocide, I returned to my house and came to learn that my friend, who had given me the house, was killed in the genocide. I went to visit her children and resumed my responsibility of delivering the money for rent to them.

It was at this time that, due to the horrific experiences I went through – gang rape, beatings, the fear and trauma – I joined the Polyclinic of Hope Centre, a RWN project for victims of rape and violent crimes. The Polyclinic of Hope started in 1995 and I was one of its first members. The Clinic is a space for interaction, provides free medical care for members and their families, trauma and HIV and AIDS counselling, care and support for PLWHA, micro-credit, information on human rights and legal aid, and education and awareness on different issues.

In 1998, because my house had been destroyed during the genocide, the RWN assisted me to rehabilitate it. I was offered materials including sand, stones, cement, paint, timber and iron sheets, as well as the labour to help in the repairs that needed to be done.

In 2000, I started receiving people claiming to be brothers of the husband of my friend, demanding that I move out of their house because the house was not mine. I refused to move out because I believed the house to be mine, although I had no documents showing that my friend had given me the house. Her children were aware of this situation and also that the family of her husband had not contributed anything to the property's acquisition. The problem continued and I was reported to the local authorities. The claimants' main strength was that I had no official document showing the house was given to me. They reported me, saying I had refused to give them their property.

I was accompanied and advised by the RWN on the day our case was to be heard and through the whole process. The authorities were not ready to believe my statement without any written document. It was only when my friend's children came forward that matters improved. They testified that they were aware of their mother having given me the house and that I was helping them manage the rest of the property in their absence. Hearing this, the local authorities decided I should stay in the house and gave me a document testifying to this decision.

The claimants were not satisfied with this decision and resolved to use other means to get me out of the house. In collaboration with my neighbours and the surrounding community involved in my genocide case, they started harassing me and my family. At night they would throw stones on the roof of my house; they would attack, beat and harass me as I came from the market where I was working. When I reported the different harassment incidents to the police, the people involved were arrested, but after about one week they were released.

After this, they were determined to do worse. They came at night with pangas and knives, started hitting on my door saying they would kill me. They were heard by some of the neighbours, one of whom was a policeman. He came with a gun and shot in the air and the assailants ran off. I reported again to the police, investigations were carried out, and arrests were made.

I was traumatised and living in fear for my life and family, so the police advised me and the RWN to find a way to relocate me for security reasons. At that time, beneficiaries for a shelter programme among women victims of violent crimes at the Polyclinic of Hope Centre were being identified, so I was included.

At the end of the construction of the 20 houses that make up the Village of Hope, I moved to my new home, the police department even providing transport. The Village of Hope was constructed by the RWN for women victims of rape and other violent crimes who had no shelter at the end of the 1994 genocide.

When I decided to rent out the house I had been staying in, the different tenants were harassed the same way I had been harassed – with stones and other objects being thrown on the roof at night. When the last tenant moved out, the house remained empty for something like two months and then the same people who had reported me before reported again to the local authorities. They claimed that I had moved out of the house, left it empty, and that the person who had given it to me without even any written document had left orphans who were suffering and could use the income from the same house to improve their welfare.

Considering the case history – no written document to show that the house was given to me, lack of security and income from the house due to the tenants being harassed out of it, the fact that I had a home to stay in now, and in consideration of my health (a woman survivor who had been gang-raped and was living with HIV and AIDS because of this) – the RWN advised me to claim for the funds invested in renovation and then allow the house to revert to the children of my friend. This is the decision the local authorities passed and the money used for renovation was given back to me.

Concurrently with the above, I was following up a case with my second husband for having deserted us, and not having provided any support to our two children. Because we were not married legally under Rwandan law, I first of all took him to court in 2002 in order that he acknowledged the children as his. Upon the decision of the court in favour of the aforementioned, my former husband was supposed to provide child support and the children would have a right to inherit their father's property. He did not fulfill his responsibilities as a father and I reported him to the local authorities. After hearing our case, the court requested my former husband to give me RWF15 000 (US$26) per month for child support.

'They came at night with pangas and knives.'

In conclusion, I would say that in order for women's rights to be protected, women need to be sensitised. They also need to be determined to demand that their rights be respected. Women also need support and reinforcement because I would have found it very difficult to follow up my cases and demand redress without the assistance of the RWN and the Polyclinic of Hope. Also, for the existing laws and structures that protect women's rights to work, women have the responsibility of coming forward.

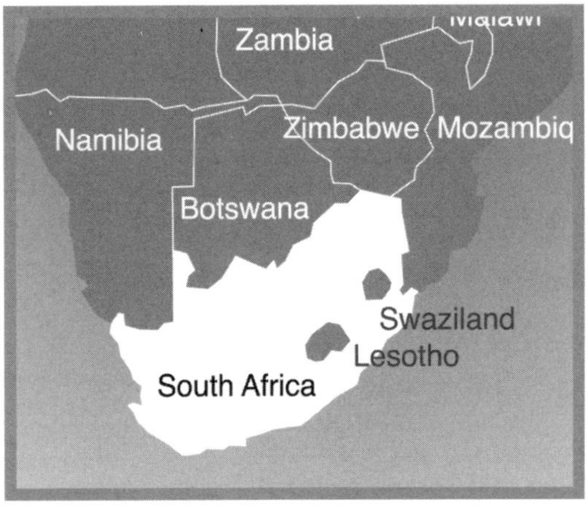

Country profile South Africa

The country has a population of 46.9 million people (UNDP 2005). It has a market economy that is largely based on services, manufacturing and mining, with a GDP per capita of US$3 489, which is one of the highest in sub-Saharan Africa. South Africa's agricultural sector is still characterised by a high degree of dualism, with large-scale commercial farms using hired labour in the commercial farming areas, and small farms operated by family labour in the communal farming areas. Agriculture uses 82.3 per cent of the total land in the country, of which grazing land makes up almost 70 per cent of all agricultural land (FAO 2003b). Agriculture contributes 3.8 per cent to the GDP and employs 8 per cent of the workforce. Mining accounts for 10 per cent of the GDP and is dominated by the production of gold.

The first multi-racial elections of 1994, shortly after the collapse of apartheid, brought the African National Congress into power, presiding over a multi-party Government of National Unity. South Africa is the most urbanised and industrialised country in sub-Saharan Africa, but with high levels of unemployment and inequality in income distribution (Walker 2002). Around 14 million South Africans, approaching one third of the total population, are vulnerable to food shortages due to the lack of suitable infrastructure in the deep rural areas (FAO 2005a).

In total, 5.3 million adults and children are living with HIV, including 2.9 million women and 230 000 children (UNAIDS 2004). By 2003, 370 000 people had died of AIDS, and the number of orphans due to AIDS is as high as 1.1 million. The 2002 data showed that 24 per cent of young pregnant women (15–24 years) in the capital city were estimated to be HIV-positive.

About 67.5 per cent of all land is privately owned commercial farm land, almost all of it white-owned, while 14 per cent of the land, the former reserves ('Bantustans'), is held by the state in trust for the people living on it, who number some 30 per cent of the population (Walker 2002). Since 1994, South Africa has been implementing land reforms whose three major components are tenure reform, land restitution and land redistribution.

The pace of land redistribution has been slow, but the restitution programme has achieved considerable progress, especially in urban areas. The Communal Land Rights Act 2004 attempts to secure the tenure rights of people living under tenure systems in the former 'Bantustans' or communal areas of South Africa, including those of women, but critics are concerned that it may weaken the rights of vulnerable members of society, including women, due to the Act's focus on placing authority over land in the hands of traditional leaders (COHRE 2004).

Under South Africa's customary legal system, succession is based on the principle of primogeniture, whereby the estate is devolved essentially through the male line only. During the constitutional negotiations, women's organisations were able to block an attempt by traditional leaders to have customary law exempted from the provisions of the Equality Clause in the Constitution (Walker 2002). The government's 1997 White Paper on Land Reform makes gender equity a basic principle and identifies women as a social category that must be targeted in land reform programmes. The land redistribution programme is open to men and women, but there are concerns that women will not be able to compete for access to land and grants on equal terms with men because of their weaker social and economic status.

The Women's Legal Centre (WLC)

The WLC was established in 1998 by a group of women lawyers. There are two major mandates of the organisation. One of them is to conduct constitutional litigation on women's rights to remove all legal barriers that prevent women's rights being achieved. The other one is to advocate law reforms to achieve women's rights. Legal advice to women on their rights is also provided. The WLC litigates cases and conducts law reform in the following areas: child sexual abuse, customary law, domestic partnerships, maintenance issues, Muslim personal law, unfair dismissal, violence against women, and women's access to resources.

These sections contain heads of arguments and other legal pleadings which have been used in previous cases argued by the WLC. Any litigation conducted by the WLC must advance substantive equality for women and have a wide impact.

The WLC performs a wide range of advocacy work, including submissions, materials developments, publications, presentations, workshops, and consultation with other NGOs and with communities.

Wola Nani

Wola Nani was established in 1994 as a non-profit organisation to help bring relief to the communities hardest hit by the HIV crisis. Formed against a background of economic curtailment on welfare spending and a huge increase in the number of HIV and AIDS cases, Wola Nani initiated programmes to help HIV-positive people in the local community cope with the emotional and financial strains brought about by HIV and AIDS.

Making the law known and enforceable

SIBONGILE NDASHE
Attorney, WLC
Interview by Kaori Izumi, March 2005

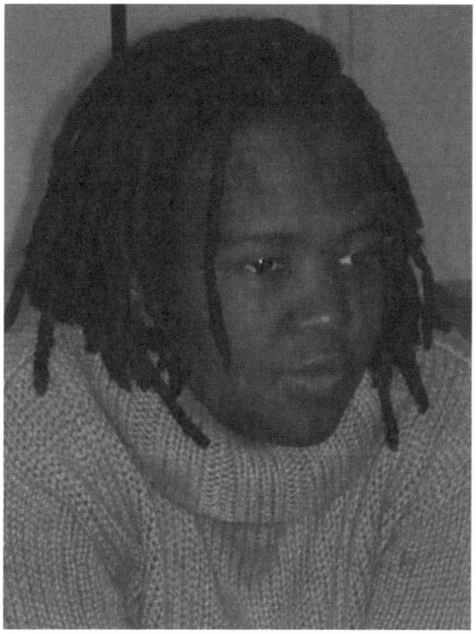

The South African Constitution provides a good normative framework to protect women's rights in general, including women's property rights. But, despite the Constitution, discrimination against women continues. We have managed to achieve several victories in strategic litigation against Muslim laws and the Black Administration Act, which had previously discriminated against women's property rights. Black laws and customs meant that only males could inherit property, but this is unconstitutional in South Africa today as it is against basic human rights and gender equality, as well as women's dignity. What makes South Africa different from other countries in the region is that in South Africa one cannot discriminate against others based on custom. Customary law is recognised in South Africa, but there is a limit placed upon it. If a customary law is not consistent with the Constitution, the Constitution overrules that law.

'In South Africa one cannot discriminate against others based on custom.'

A discrepancy exists between what the law says and what is practised. We need laws, but often laws are badly drafted and also bad in content. People are resistant to new laws and the state is often not able to deal with this resistance. If widows are evicted, there is no way of enforcing their entitlement provided by the law; the law is useless. Although women say, 'We have the rights', devolution of property and transfer of land laws need the means to enforce the rights. Women need to have access to the judiciary in order to make the law enforceable.

When the law is not certain or people do not understand it, there are more chances for discrimination against women and property-grabbing to take place. If it is not generally known that discrimination based on sex is not sanctioned by law, it increases the vulnerability of women.

The issue of HIV and AIDS and property-grabbing is not systematically documented in South Africa because of the stigma attached to HIV and AIDS. We only hear about isolated cases. Evictions are happening, not only to widows, but to child-headed households as well. As our organisation mainly works in urban areas, we have little information on what is happening with these issues in rural areas.

HIV and AIDS increase vulnerability. People do not want to be associated with HIV and AIDS. Violence against HIV-positive people is an issue in South Africa. Gutu Dlamini's murder case illustrates how HIV-positive people are stigmatised and victimised. HIV is a death sentence for people living in poverty. Where there is no support available, what is the point of disclosing your status? If you disclose, people look at you with disapproval and they discriminate against you. So there is no interest in disclosing your status. People are being evicted, but there is little evidence to link the relationship between HIV and AIDS and property-grabbing or evictions. In South Africa, it is difficult to detect a pattern of property-grabbing related to HIV and AIDS.

The most important issue concerning women's property rights is to ensure that laws are properly implemented and people, that is, women, communities, traditional leaders, magistrates' offices, etc., are made aware of the existing laws which punish discrimination against women. There is a need for people to understand the law, just as there is a need for the law to remain consistent in content and application.

Lack of women's property rights increases vulnerability for women and their children, as it makes them more vulnerable to poverty and domestic violence. As a consequence, women become more vulnerable to HIV infection and AIDS. This is the vicious circle that needs to be broken.

Overcoming the stigma of HIV and AIDS

NOMAWETHU SHUMANI
Wola Nani
Interview by Sibongile Ndashe, March 2005

I found out I was HIV-positive in 1994 when I tried to join my husband's health policy. I was rejected and advised to see my doctor. He told me I was HIV-positive, but when he saw my wedding ring he told me there had probably been a mistake and he would check. But there wasn't. My husband was tested soon afterwards and he too was found to be positive. I did not receive any counselling at this stage and did not understand. I did not know about HIV. I thought it could be treated.

My husband blamed me for infecting him and accused me of cheating. We argued a lot. Then, at Somerset Hospital, we were given some counselling and began to understand a little about HIV and how to live with it. We recognised the need to support each other. But it was very hard. My husband was unfaithful a lot and had many girlfriends. He would disappear for weeks and months at a time. He abused me, said that I had cheated on him, and he threatened to kill me if I told anyone. He didn't want people to know about our status because he thought it would stop him getting more girlfriends.

I did not want to tell anyone. I kept quiet. I was in denial. It was a bad time for me. No food, no electricity, no money, nothing. I was alone, depressed, sick. I closed the doors and pretended not to be there. I was in a dark room. Then I got a casual job at the Post Office. My husband came back and took the money. He began to abuse me again. He did everything. If my hair was short you could see the scars on my head where he stabbed me. I reported him to the police, but my husband was a policeman and they took no notice of me. Eventually I went to court, where they listened and my husband was sent to prison for nine months.

The job at the Post Office became permanent. Life was getting better, but I still did not tell anyone about my status. I didn't want anyone to know, especially in my workplace. So when the Post Office introduced an insurance scheme, I did not go. People began to get suspicious because I also did not donate blood, even when they offered you free tea and a biscuit during your lunch break. 'Why does Noma not go for the insurance and give blood?' they would ask. Then my friend got a job at the Post Office. She knows me well and I knew she would suspect, so I left. I pretended to have found a good job elsewhere.

But I did not have a job to go to. I went home and my husband would beat and abuse me. With no money and no job I turned to a friend who is a social worker and confided in her. She suggested I apply for a job with Child Welfare and, with my experience and driving licence, I got the job. But just a few months later I told a colleague I had shingles and she said it could be related to HIV. I was scared they would know, so I left the next day.

Life was very bad. I was very depressed at home. I had only a half-loaf of bread a week from a food parcel. This was not enough. I became very sick. My husband locked me in a dark room with no food and left me there. I was very ill. I had diarrhoea. I had no choice but to use the Hoover as a toilet. It was very bad. But my neighbours heard me banging on the wall and helped me. I had been in that room for about three days. Then I went to hospital.

When I came home, I avoided my family and friends. I could not tell them and I wanted to be alone. I went to see the doctor about the shingles. The door was wide open and the receptionist and the waiting room full of people could hear what he said. He talked about HIV openly, in front of them. I was very angry. He is not supposed to tell anyone. The receptionist knows me and she told my family. I went to the AIDS Training, Information & Counselling Centre to complain. How could I sue the doctor? But here I found out about Wola Nani ('we embrace and develop one another') in Khayelitsha. I decided not to sue and rather concentrate on myself.

I was very scared of Wola Nani at first. I did not know about the counselling and support group. I was worried they would tell people I am HIV-positive. But they give you a free cup of coffee and a piece of bread. At home each night alone, I would think, 'I don't want to go', but in the morning I would think of the coffee and bread and would go. They would talk about the virus, but I didn't want to talk with them and was always giggling and chatting. The counsellor was HIV-positive and she didn't know me. Still I was not sure, but then I found myself thinking each night, 'Tomorrow at Wola Nani I will be with people I can talk to and who will support me … when I'm there, I know I am free.' I became friends with the other people and the staff. I felt I belonged. I even became a volunteer and then became a project assistant on the income-generation scheme.

I realised I wanted to disclose my status and help educate others so they could protect themselves. It was three years after I had first found out about my HIV status. But first I had to divorce my husband. So, one day at the clinic, when it was very crowded and there were many people, I said to myself, 'Today is the day. I am sick and tired of hiding this. I need people to support me.' I publicly told everyone and shared my HIV status with the people there. Under apartheid I had been an activist and in Khayelitsha people knew me. After my announcement, news quickly spread and the local radio station, Radio Zibonele, asked to interview me. I was ready. I wanted people to know. I wanted them to understand. Protect yourselves: this is what I told my family.

Then the discrimination began. People would point at me in the street and say, 'You must not go near Noma's house or you will get HIV.' At a party, I noticed people were very odd with me and I heard someone say, 'Be careful, she is spreading the virus in this area ... cover your glass so she can't put blood in your drink.' My father-in-law threatened to sue me if I used my married name. And then my nieces and nephews asked me not to use my maiden name as people would think they too had HIV. So I became just Noma.

But now, things are different. HIV is everywhere and more accepted. The people who would not speak to me now send their children for advice and counselling. I am glad I can help. It is important to educate people so they can protect themselves and they can live well. I am happy now. I have accepted my HIV status. Life is good and I am well. I married again in December 2002. I think I am a role model.

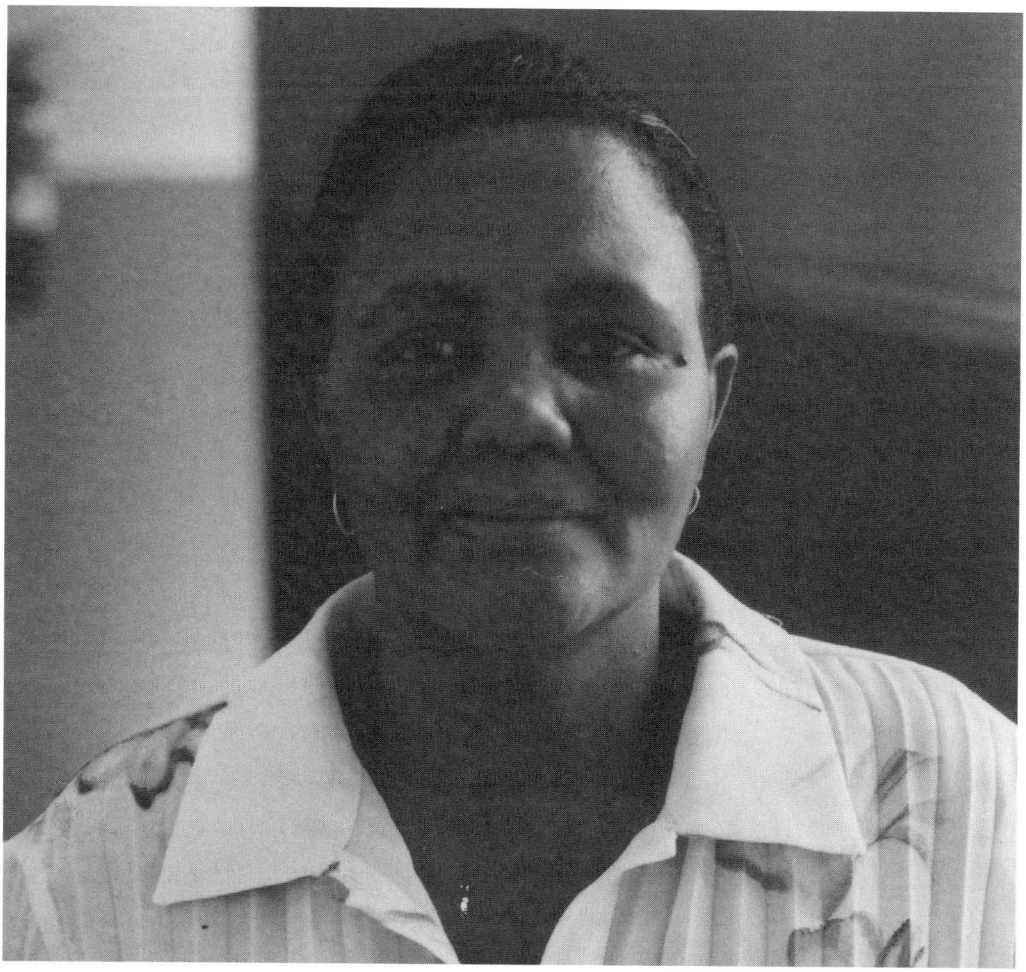

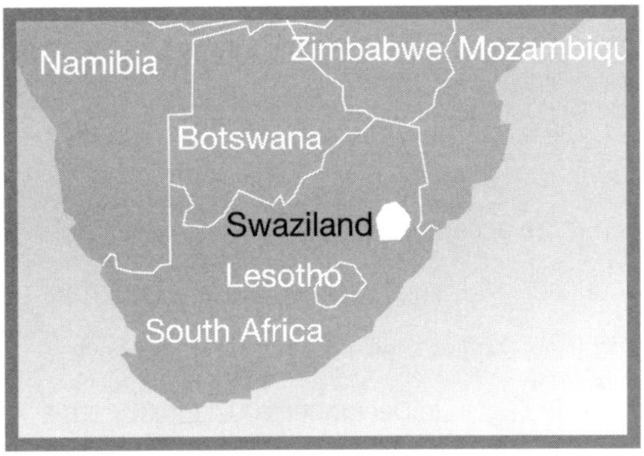

County profile Swaziland

Swaziland is a small landlocked kingdom in southern Africa governed by an absolute monarchy, where succession is based on custom. The country has a population of one million people, the demographics of which have been significantly affected by the rapid spread of HIV and AIDS (FAO 2003c). Life expectancy is as low as 32.5 years old (UNDP 2005). It is estimated that the present population is 30 000 people (3 per cent) fewer than it would have been without the pandemic.

Swaziland is a lower-middle income country with a GDP per capita of US$1 669 (FAO 2003c). The country is heavily dependent on South Africa for imports and exports. Customs duties from the Southern African Customs Union and worker remittances from South Africa substantially supplement domestically earned income. Primary production, mainly agriculture, accounted for only 9 per cent of the GDP in 2001. In 2002, the estimated poverty incidence for Swaziland was 66 per cent. Income is unevenly distributed in Swaziland and inequality exists in access to assets such as cattle and land, and between urban and rural areas (World Bank 1995).

In total, of 220 000 adults and children living with HIV and AIDS, 110 000 are adult women and 16 000 are children (UNAIDS 2004). By 2003, 17 000 people had died of AIDS, creating, as a result, 65 000 orphans. In the capital city, Mbabane, 39 per cent of young pregnant women were estimated to be HIV-positive in 2002.

Land tenure is broadly of two types, Swazi National Lands and Title Deed Land, which account for 54 and 46 per cent of land area respectively (FAO 2005b). Tenure over Swazi National Land is not defined by legislation, the land being controlled and held in trust by the King and allocated by tribal chiefs according to traditional arrangements. There is a structural divide between large-scale Title Deed Land and small-scale Swazi National Land with its predominantly smallholder agriculture. According to the 94/95 Agriculture Census, 61 per cent of Swazi National Land farm holdings are less than one hectare in size. Most farms are thus very small. The rapid population increase is, in turn, exerting pressure on land availability for cropping and grazing, forcing households to produce crops on increasingly fragile lands.

According to Swazi tradition, inheritance issues should be handled by the deceased's family and heir and should not be challenged, especially not by a woman. Under customary law, women cannot own property, enter into contracts or represent themselves in court, as they are considered to be legal minors. Married women are generally subject to the marital power of their husbands, under both customary and civil forms of marriage, unless they are among the very small group of women who are married under civil law and have taken steps to specify that the marriage is out of community of property (WLSA 1997). The draft Land Policy does make some cautious nods in the direction of gender equity at the level of principle, by advocating the removal of land-related legal impediments to gender equity in customary tenure (Walker 2002). The draft National Policy is still under review. The prime objectives of the draft policy are the realisation of human rights, the promotion of gender equality, and the protection of property rights.

Swazis Positive Living (SWAPOL)

SWAPOL was established in 2001 by five HIV-positive women experiencing stigma and discrimination from their in-laws and community members. The organisation currently has over a thousand members, who are people living with HIV and AIDS (PLWHA), and is supporting 30 communities. In each community where it works, the mission of SWAPOL is to provide support to improve the quality of life for PLWHA and people affected by HIV and AIDS in an effective and efficient manner. Their work includes:

- Providing training and education in HIV and AIDS to rural communities;
- Promoting positive living and good nutrition to rural communities;
- Providing counselling services to grieving families;
- Establishing income-generating projects in rural communities;
- Taking care of the terminally ill patients in rural communities.

Nutrition is one of the components that is needed for an HIV-positive person to boost the weakened immune system. Family gardens have been set up and continuously promoted for use by HIV-positive people. SWAPOL organises PLWHA and caregivers in growing vegetables in backyard gardens in order to access nutrition at household level. The organisation also promotes food security for households of PLWHA and orphans.

Many PLWHA, in particular orphans and widows, have been left behind with no source of income or survival skills. This programme empowers PLWHA with sustainable skills that impact on their socio-economic status and improve their livelihoods. PLWHA identify their projects, for example, vegetable gardens, cash-crop farming, sewing school uniforms, etc. Orphans and vulnerable children are secondary beneficiaries of such programmes. A quarter of the profit from these projects goes to a community trust fund for orphans.

Eleven hectares of maize have been planted at Mahlangatsha. This project enables female PLWHA to access nutritious mealie-meal and to sell the maize to earn a living. They also grow crops like groundnuts, jugo beans, beans, sweet potatoes and potatoes.

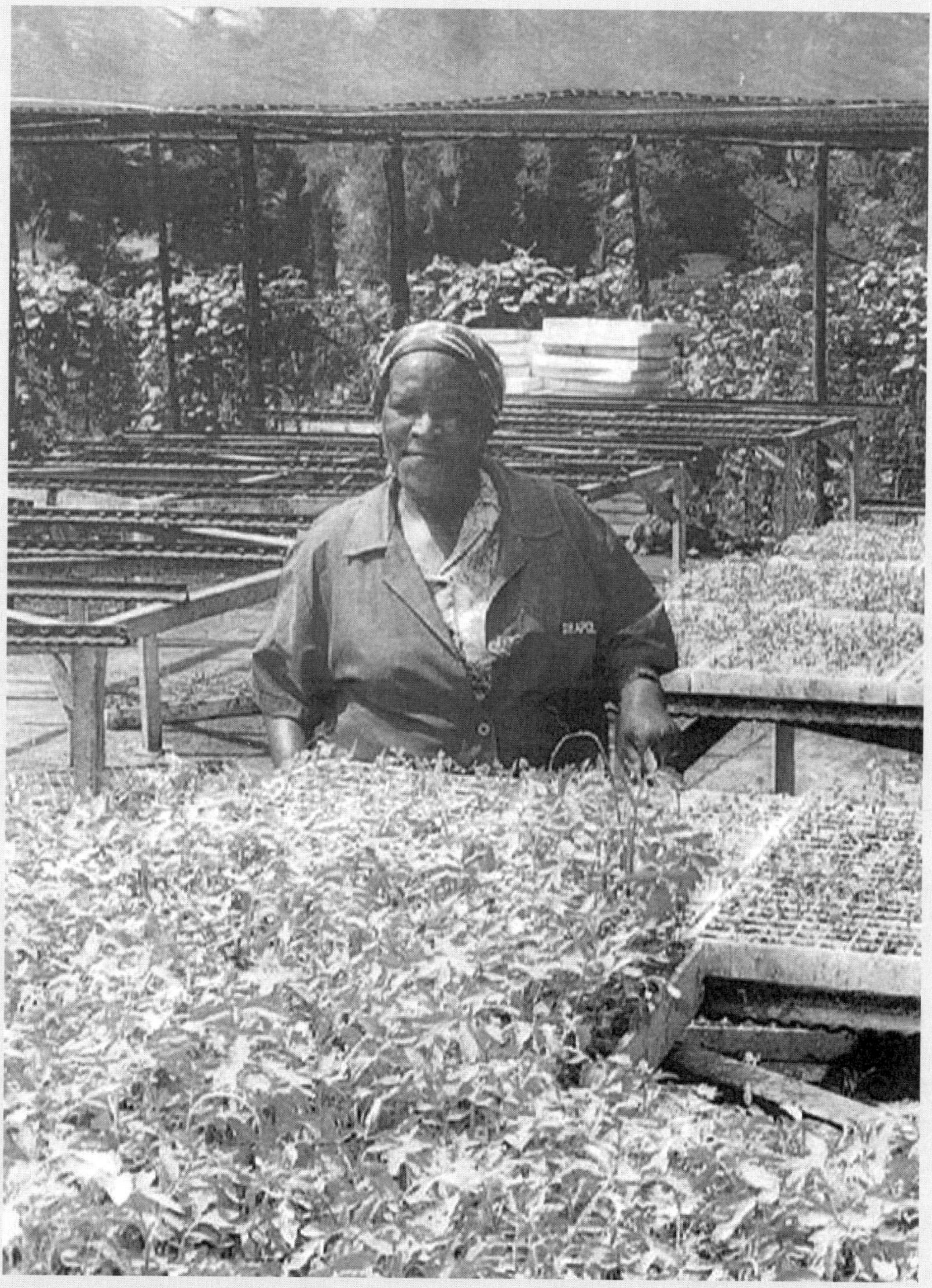

SWAPOL's agricultural cooperatives

SIPHIWE HLOPHE
Director, SWAPOL
Interview conducted by Kaori Izumi on 30 March, Harare, and on 7 July, Windhoek, 2005

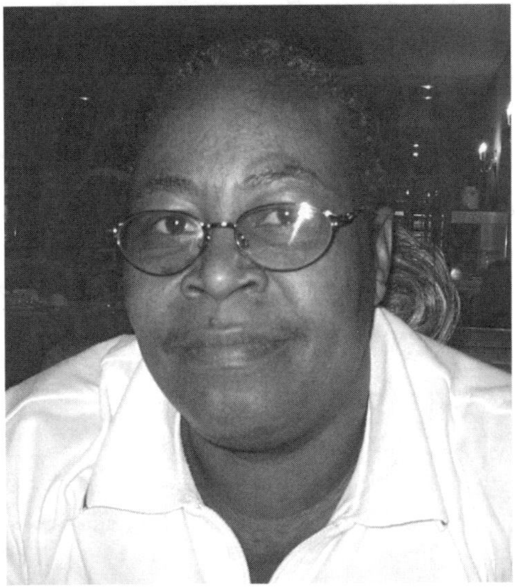

I started the organisation with four other women in May 2001. It was myself, Siphiwe Hlophe, Thelma Dlamini, Ellen Hlatshwako, Nohlanhla Dlamini, and Gugu Mbatha.

Thelma was working at the Deputy Prime Minister's Office. She fell ill, decided to go for testing and found out she was HIV-positive. She told her husband and he deserted her. She told her in-laws, too. They also blamed her for bringing the disease home. They meant that she had a lover outside the marriage. They never wanted to talk to her, because they feared that she would infect others at home. Then her husband also got sick and he died. Her in-laws accused her of having infected him. At his funeral, she was sitting alone at the corner, deserted. She had six children. She moved to her government house. She did not inherit anything because her in-laws refused to let her take any property. Thelma passed away at the age of 40 in May 2005.

Her children were scattered. I took the first three children to look after – they were 15, 16 and 18 years old. I took other two children, who were 6 and 8 years old, to the 'Save our Sons' orphanage, because I could not take them. We are still struggling to take the benefits of their father's and mother's pension for the children. Because her in-laws do not want to talk to us, they tell us that we have finished the story a long time ago. I have not been able to get their mother's pension for the children because I am not a relative, says the Master of the High Court. Thelma's mother also passed away. I am still struggling to get their pensions for their children. I have four children of my own. I have my late sister's three orphans. I also have three children from another of our members who died. I have 13 children in my house altogether.

Ellen is 50 years old. She was a cleaner at a government office. Her husband was working in the mine and he was sick with the symptoms of HIV. Ellen's mother-in-law told her that Ellen had her husband and a lover, so she (Ellen) wanted the husband to die. When her husband died, he was taken away from her and buried at his parents' home. She did not get a pension from his mine employers. But because the in-laws would not grab the property of a 'witch', she retained her house with her two children. She is a chairperson for our income-generating project.

Nohlanhla is 39 years old. Her husband is a mine worker. She was a cleaner at a clerical office. She got pregnant, but fell ill and she was tested positive. She told her mother-in-law about her HIV status. When her husband came back from the mine, the family had a meeting. After the meeting they sent her to her parents' home because they said she had brought the virus to the family. When we started the organisation, her baby got ill and passed away. She had five children, but they were taken away by her in-laws. After we started the organisation, we made sure that our family should be educated on HIV. Her husband came to ask her to come back. Because of HIV, her in-laws did not want to stay with her and gave them a piece of plot at their homestead, so that Nohlanhla and the husband could build their own house. Nohlanhla was retrenched, but now she is responsible for our vegetable project.

Gugu passed away in 2002. She was only 27 years old. We were doing a project in her community. Her mother was a rural health motivator. I wanted to see her mother to get some information. When I visited her mother's house, I saw Gugu sitting at the corner. When she saw me, she ran away. I asked her why she was hiding. She said that she did not want to see people. Once, I visited her when she was alone at home. Then Gugu told me that she was HIV-positive. She told me that each time when she went out, people pointed at her. I told her that I was also HIV-positive. I told her, 'We have to do something. We are sharing stigma and discrimination from our in-laws. We will start an organisation.'

Our first meeting was at Gugu's house. We discussed a need to educate families on HIV and AIDS, to start income-generating activities to improve the standard of living of HIV-positive women, and to pass knowledge to their families and communities where they resided. Our members' primary concern was how to live positively. SWAPOL contacted UNICEF who agreed to support our activities.

I talked to Allen Brody, the UNICEF representative in Swaziland. I told him that we had a problem of HIV and AIDS in rural communities. I told him that we face discrimination, we are chased away by our in-laws, and that we are not accepted. I asked him, 'Since you have a programme on community action on child rights, can you give us a support that we could do to educate our own rural folks on HIV and AIDS?' He agreed and supported us. He exposed us internationally. He made sure that Stephen Lewis[12] would visit our project when he came to Swaziland.

One of our orphans is HIV-positive. We are starting a new project on home-based care especially for children. Swaziland has a high infection rate of HIV; the latest figure is almost over 40 per cent.

UNICEF developed a string game on how HIV is passing within a family, relatives and country, which we will use for sensitisation.

I was a project manager at the extension section of the Ministry of Agriculture and I was involved in project promotion and income-generation activities for farmers. I worked at the Ministry of Agriculture up to 2003. Only since 2003, I have been working full time with SWAPOL.

Today, the membership of the organisation is 1 003, covering 30 rural communities in Swaziland. Of the 1 003 members, 55 per cent are widows, separated and single women. A support group was established in each community with seven committee members. We mobilised local leaders, such as the chief, council, pastor and churches, and community police, to support people living with HIV and AIDS (PLWHA).

Our activities include: community sensitisation on HIV and AIDS, promotion of improved nutrition for PLWHA, nutrition gardening, income-generating activities, sewing school uniforms for contracts with schools, training of family caregivers, providing food aid to HIV and AIDS patients and orphans, offering assistance to abused children and widows, home-based care, and setting up neighbourhood care points for orphans and vulnerable children. In the past years, we organised 110 child-protection committees in rural communities and stepped up the training and placement of community counsellors to assist AIDS orphans, widows and PLWHA. We also recommend that everybody should have a nutrition garden. The organisation also does training on business management, including record-keeping. We conduct monitoring visits on production and sales of products by each support group.

Stigma against HIV and AIDS is a serious problem, whereby an HIV-positive person is not allowed to use the same dish as her or his family, and their children are not allowed to play with other children.

Most of our members are without jobs, either retrenched or lying at home.

In November 2001, we started to negotiate with chiefs for a piece of land. It was difficult to convince chiefs why our women needed a piece of land. It took a long time to make them understand it. We kept visiting chiefs to talk about land issues and finally managed to get two chiefs to support our idea. A female chief, Nconyi Dlamini, supported our idea, I think because she was a woman and she had orphans. She convinced other chiefs. In February 2002, we managed to acquire 11 hectares of land in Mahlangatsha, 40 km southeast of the capital, Mbabane. So far, 13 out of 30 of our support groups have acquired a piece of land from a chief where the members are farming legumes, maize and tubers. Our plan is to get more land.

In the 2003/2004 season, we harvested 300 bags of maize; 50 bags were put into storage for emergencies; 5 bags were given to the neighbourhood care points, where orphans and vulnerable children received meals twice a day; and 10 bags were delivered to child-headed households run by teenagers who had lost their parents due to AIDS. The rest of the maize was sold for US$3 883. For last season, 2004/2005, we planted vegetables, groundnuts, potatoes and sweet potatoes and beans.

We have experienced at least five cases where a widow was not allowed to continue the use of a farming plot after the husband had died. In Swaziland, unless a woman has a boy child or she gets consent from in-laws or her own brothers, she needs to keep begging for a piece of land until the day she dies. Cases of women who are evicted from rural homes are frequently reported by the media, but they are not properly documented.

We have one widow living who is HIV-positive. Her husband died of HIV and AIDS. Her brother-in-law, who was the head of the family, was controlling everything that was left by her deceased husband. When her husband was still alive, they had planted fruit trees. After her husband had died, one day, when she tried to eat the fruits, her brother-in-law decided to cut all the fruit trees so that she would not get the fruits. When she tried to communicate with her brother-in-law, asking why he was doing it to her, he told her that she had killed his brother and she was the one who brought the virus home, because she was not faithful to her husband. She decided to report the matter to the local council, but the council told her that the case was a family matter. She was told to return back and sort out the issue with her in-laws. Property-grabbing from widows is an area we need to work on in the future.

'Our members' primary concern was how to live positively.'

Now we are left with only three of us, Ellen, Nohlanhla and me. After all that I have experienced, I changed my attitude and thinking. Since I started the organisation, I needed to be a role model for all women living with HIV, for all the women encountering problems. I need to live up to assist them. I do not think of my HIV status anymore. I need to live long for the sake of our women. If I die, other women will die. This is how I am feeling. In our meetings, our members say, 'We are all praying that you will not die before us. Because, if you die, we do not know what to do.' There is no cell-counting machine in Swaziland. So I go to Johannesburg every two months. My cell is 500. I am not on antiretroviral therapy.

Country profile **Tanzania**

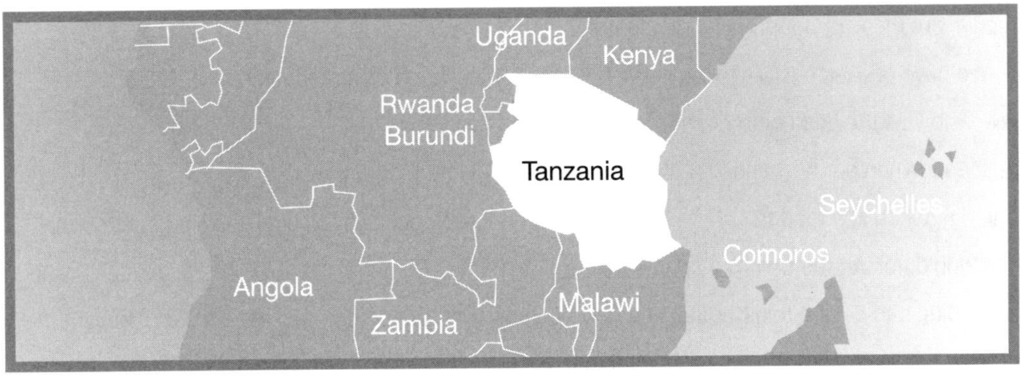

The United Republic of Tanzania consists of the mainland and Zanzibar. Tanzania is one of the poorest countries in the world with a GDP per capita of US$249 (UNDP 2005). The country has a population of 36.9 million, of which 63 per cent live in rural areas. Food insecurity is a major problem in Tanzania. Flood, drought, and inefficient internal markets often cause severe food shortages in areas where people live under the poverty line (Save the Children UK 2005). The agricultural sector continues to lead the economy, providing work for 79 per cent of the economically active population, where women play a major role.

In Tanzania, 1.6 million adults and children, including 140 000 adult women and 60 000 children, are estimated to be living with HIV (UNAIDS 2004). It is predicted that the mean age of the working population (labour force) will decline from 31.5 to 29 years between 1992 and 2010. It is further estimated that AIDS will reduce the average real GDP growth rate in the period 1985–2010 from 3.9 per cent, without AIDS, to between 2.8 and 3.3 per cent with AIDS (TACAIDS n.d.).

Tanzania's Constitution lacks crucial provisions declaring women's equal inheritance rights (UN-HABITAT 2002). While the Law on Marriage Act of 1971 gives women a stronger position in marriage and co-habitation, it still does not amount to women's equal rights. The 1991 Commission of

Inquiry identified problems in women's access to land, especially with regard to succession and inheritance (Walker 2002). The 1997 Land Policy is ambiguous with regard to women's rights in terms of customary law – it confirms that women should have legal rights to own land but that inheritance of clan land should be in terms of customary law, provided that this is not in conflict with the Constitution. It also proposes that the ownership of land between husband and wife should not be subject to legislation but that family land should not be disposed of without the consent of both spouses.

In 1999, a Land Act and a Village Land Act were passed. The Village Land Act designates Village Councils to administer village land. The Land Act specifically declares that women have the same rights as men to acquire, own and deal in land. It also provides that where land is held in the name of one spouse, the other spouse has a presumed right of occupancy and that the disposal of land not consented to by both spouses is invalid (Walker 2002). The Village Land Act authorises the Village Council to allocate land and specifies that at least one third of its total of 25 members should be women, and that a quorum of four members must have at least two women. It also establishes Village Adjudication Committees to deal with disputes and provides that the interests of women, absentees and the disabled should be safeguarded (Walker 2002).

The key challenge in Tanzania is not only to make the rural people, especially women, know and understand their land rights, but to facilitate access to them by providing appropriate documentation and training.

Land of our own

PELAGIA KATUNZI
HIV and AIDS counsellor, Kagera, Tanzania
Presented at the FAO/HSRC Regional Workshop on HIV and AIDS and Land Issues in Southern and East Africa, Pretoria, June 2001

The first AIDS cases in Tanzania were reported in 1983 from the Kagera Region, in the north-western part of the country. Kagera is one of 20 regions of mainland Tanzania.

Traditionally, Kagera people have always depended on farming, the main crops being bananas, the staple food, and coffee as a cash crop. They normally intercrop bananas and coffee, which are perennial crops. Land with such crops is traditionally inherited and therefore used by the same clan from one generation to the next. When a young man marries, his father divides the land and gives a portion of the land to the son, who then settles with his family. In the case where a young man dies before his parents, two things normally happen: the widow can use the land, if she has mainly male children, or the widow can be chased away if she has no male children. The children can either go with their mother or remain behind to be cared for by the grandparents. This is done so as to make sure that the plot is under the control of the husband's parents.

'The widow can be chased away if she has no male children.'

If the woman is chased away, then she, and in some cases the orphans too, suffers due to the lack of land. When she decides to return to her own clan, she does not inherit land there either, because the land has already been divided and given to her brothers. This traditional method of land tenure results in women having no land to inherit because the family assumes that when married she will inherit her husband's estate. In cases where the woman is barren, she will be chased away outright after her husband's death, even if they bought the land together. This system causes injustice, mostly to widows and orphans. On the other hand, if a woman dies before her husband, the man will normally remarry, using the excuse of needing someone to take care of him and the children. This habit acts as another means of spreading HIV and AIDS. No wonder there is a larger number of women contracting HIV and AIDS compared to the number of men in the same age group (assuming that the incubation period is the same in both men and women).

I have met a number of widows who were chased away, together with their children, from their land, just because they did not bear male children. The female children are expected to marry or look after themselves. This land tenure system therefore leads to many young girls ending up in prostitution or being engaged as housekeepers, factors behind the increased number of HIV and AIDS cases.

I have also experienced in my work as a counsellor that men whose wives die due to HIV and AIDS do not want to confess that their wives died from HIV and AIDS. And, when counselled and advised not to remarry, they say that a man cannot live without a wife. In cases where the new wife is young and the husband dies before her, then the stepchild(ren) might chase the woman from the land, saying it is their land inherited from their father. I have also experienced seeing widows and orphans being disadvantaged, as compared to widowers. My experience has been that land in my areas, traditionally, is owned by men and not by women.

Tanzania amended its land tenure system in 1999 by enacting a new law allowing equal ownership of land between men and women. However, it looks like this law is on paper only. It is not yet accepted by many, especially people in rural areas. Therefore, I suggest that communities should be empowered. This can be done by raising awareness through seminars and meetings, where people can be helped to understand, accept and practise according to this new law.

No boy child, no land

ZAWADI KAATANO

Interview by Pelagia Katunzi, Kagera, May 2001

My name is Zawadi Kaatano. I am 42 years old and a mother of four daughters who have borne three grandsons. In 1994, I went for a blood test to establish my health status after being attacked by a series of illnesses. The doctors told me that I had contracted the deadly HIV virus. Four years later, in 1998, my beloved husband died, leaving me with my four daughters. I was the second wife to my husband. The first wife was blessed to have six children, five males and one female. According to the traditions and cultures of the Kagera people, each male was given a piece of land to own as an inheritance and was given responsibility to take care of one of his sisters. As I had no male child I was not considered in this process of land distribution together with my children. Due to this fact I was forced to leave my house for my father's house and leave my children to be taken care of by their brothers. But this was not possible. First of all, their brothers were too young to be able to take care of them. Therefore, it was not possible to leave my children behind without any help. As I was not on good terms with the first wife, it was not possible for her to let her sons take care of my children. Additionally, the house in which I was married was given to one male child. Therefore, I had to leave with my children and go to my father's house where I was born.

My brothers welcomed me home, but with very difficult conditions. They claimed that they only knew me as their sister, but I was no longer of the 'same blood' as theirs. I felt terribly bad and angry. But since I had nowhere to go, I stayed with them for only one week. Then I left for a nearby town. There I met with a friend of mine whom I'd last met nine years ago.

My friend welcomed me so warmly that I felt as if I was at home. She was living alone, due to the fact that she was barren. She was kicked out by her husband simply because she didn't conceive. She was earning a living through selling local brew. Through her help, I managed to engage myself in casual labour on a farm near the town. My friend helped me also to secure a room where I stayed with my children. During the evening, after my farm work, I joined my friend in selling local brews. I brought up my kids in this kind of situation. I believe the environment we lived in contributed very much to the present situation. As a result of this environment, all of my children have been made pregnant by unknown men, without getting married. This is too much for me because I don't even know the fathers of my grandsons. I hear that they were pregnant by married men who cannot marry them. I found myself being a grandmother before my time, and this is only because I didn't have the opportunity to inherit a piece of land.

When I started attending counselling sessions with World Vision in Kagera, I was very much encouraged. I came to realise that there were a lot of women who were in a situation like mine, but who still struggled to overcome and live on. We are desperate and hopeless simply because the society thinks that we have no right to own the land. Our own future and that of our children are dashed, but nobody seems to care.

Country profile **Uganda**

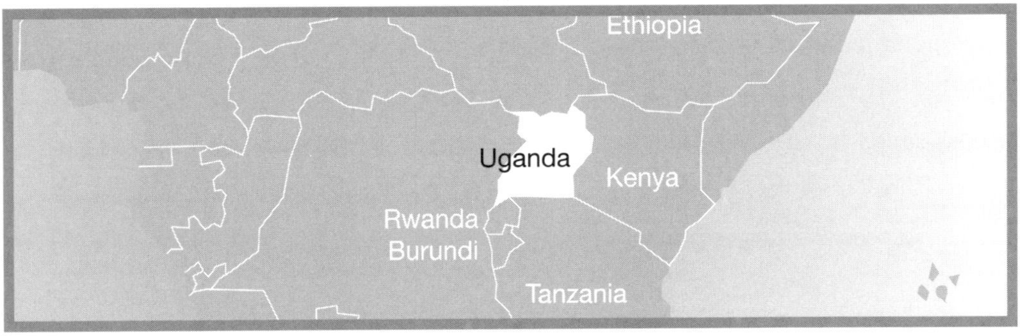

Uganda is a landlocked country in East Africa with a population of 26.9 million (UNDP 2005). The country's economy is predominantly supported by agriculture, which contributes about 41 per cent of the GDP. The agricultural sector accounts for about 85 per cent of exports and 80 per cent of the employed household population. There are about 3 million smallholder farm households, of which 80 per cent have fewer than 4 hectares of farmland. The hand-hoe is the predominant technology for cultivation. The GDP per capita is US$249. About 35 per cent of Uganda's population live on less than one dollar a day and the majority (96 per cent) of the poor live in rural areas (FAO 2003d). Politically, the country suffered a long period of civil war and destabilisation.

In Uganda, 530 000 adults and children are living with HIV, including 270 000 adult women and 89 000 children (UNAIDS 2004). By 2003, 89 000 people had died of AIDS, and 940 000 children have been orphaned due to the disease. The HIV-prevalence rate in young and pregnant women was reported to be 10 per cent in 2001. Uganda has managed to reduce the HIV-prevalence rate from 14 per cent in 1995 to 6.1 per cent in 2000, but in the areas where most of the families are child-headed due to HIV and AIDS, agricultural production has been devastated (FAO 2003d).

The Land Act of 1998 has brought into effect the land reforms agreed upon in the 1995 Constitution. Any person, family or community holding land under customary tenure on former public land may acquire a certificate of customary ownership in respect of that land, and this is convertible into freehold (Bosworth 2002). The Land Act, however, still remains to be implemented to bring about the desired changes and improvements in the land tenure systems, land policy and registration, and land administration.

The debate on women's land rights has been dominated by co-ownership of land by spouses and consent to land transactions on family land by family members. Unlike widowers, widows are only ensured of their continued occupation of the residential property they used to occupy with their husband and do not have the right to control this property in any way. The laws protect widows from eviction: the eviction of a widow from the property she has lived on with her husband before he died is clearly illegal, as is 'widow inheritance'. Women's equal rights to purchase, lease or rent land and housing in Uganda are implicitly recognised and, in addition, customary laws and traditions discriminating against women may no longer be applied. The consent clause in the Land Act of 1998 gives legally married women some control over their right to the land they occupy with their spouse.

The Government's alternative proposal to protect women's land rights through a proposed Domestic Relations Bill was not accepted by gender activists, who believed that the provision should be in the Land Act as well (Walker 2002). The Bill would, however, provide women and girls greater equality in matters related to marriage, divorce and family property. The Bill has languished in parliament for more than a decade, and it was again postponed in May 2005.

The Bunono-Ihunga Association for Women Living with HIV and AIDS

Rukungiri district is located in South-Western Province in Uganda, near the Rwanda and Congo border which is 400 km from Kampala. The area is characterised by high land pressure with a high level of land transactions, including land sales and leases. The major crops grown are bananas (as the major food and cash crop), beans, Irish potatoes and green vegetables.

The group was started in 1997 with 9 women. The total membership increased to 32, but 8 members died between 1997 and 2002. At least 3 more members died between 2002 and 2005. When their husbands died of AIDS, the women were tested positive and received counselling at Kisiizi Hospital by counsellors. They decided to form a group and named it the Bunono-Ihunga Association for Women Living with HIV and AIDS. The group has 24 women members. It has one pig and three goats, bought with money generated from basket-making. Their next objective is to buy materials for an animal shelter. The group is engaged in group savings and managed to open a group bank account.
The objectives of the association are:

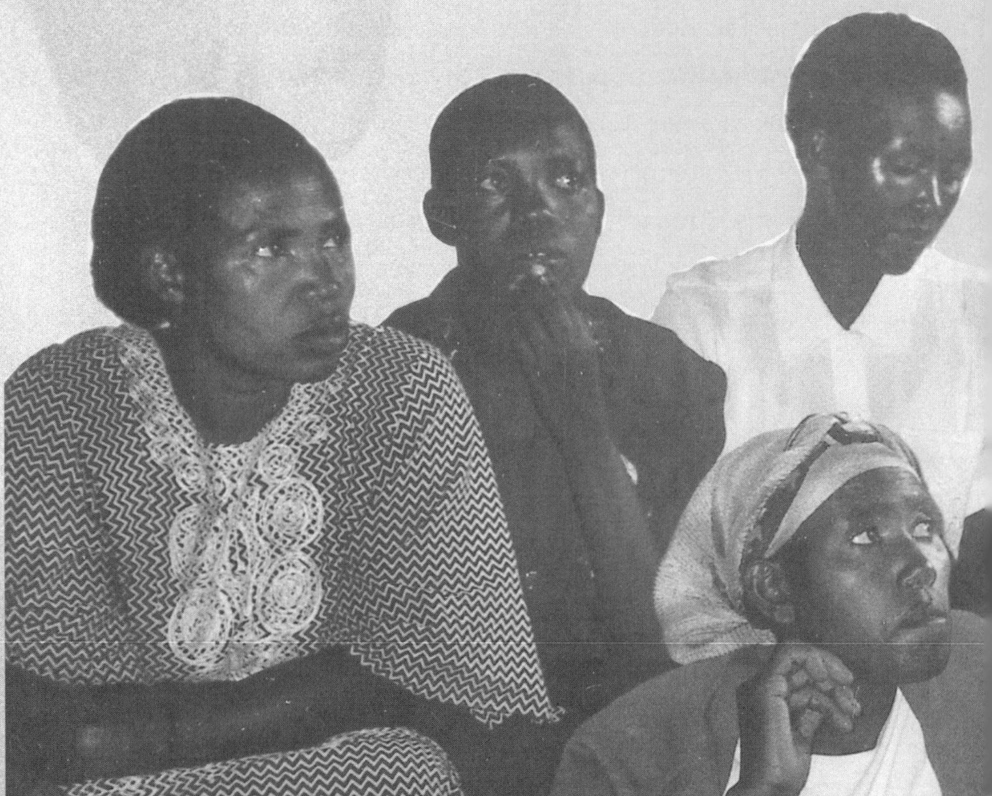

- Uniting and helping each other and sharing together everyone's problems;
- Coming together, guiding and counselling other people, and also controlling ourselves in order not to affect others;
- Sensitising others on how to avoid HIV infection and the importance of testing;
- Forming a society for sharing money for buying homes and properties;
- Looking after ourselves and our children health-wise while we are still alive.

The group assists sick members of the group; it also conducts sensitisation at churches and schools through rallies and home visits. The group drafted a script and performed a drama on HIV and AIDS at a District Council Office during an event for International AIDS Day in 2002. Some members have been trained as counsellors for HIV and AIDS patients. The constitution of the group states: 'We are determined to work together to look after ourselves and our children while we are still alive.'

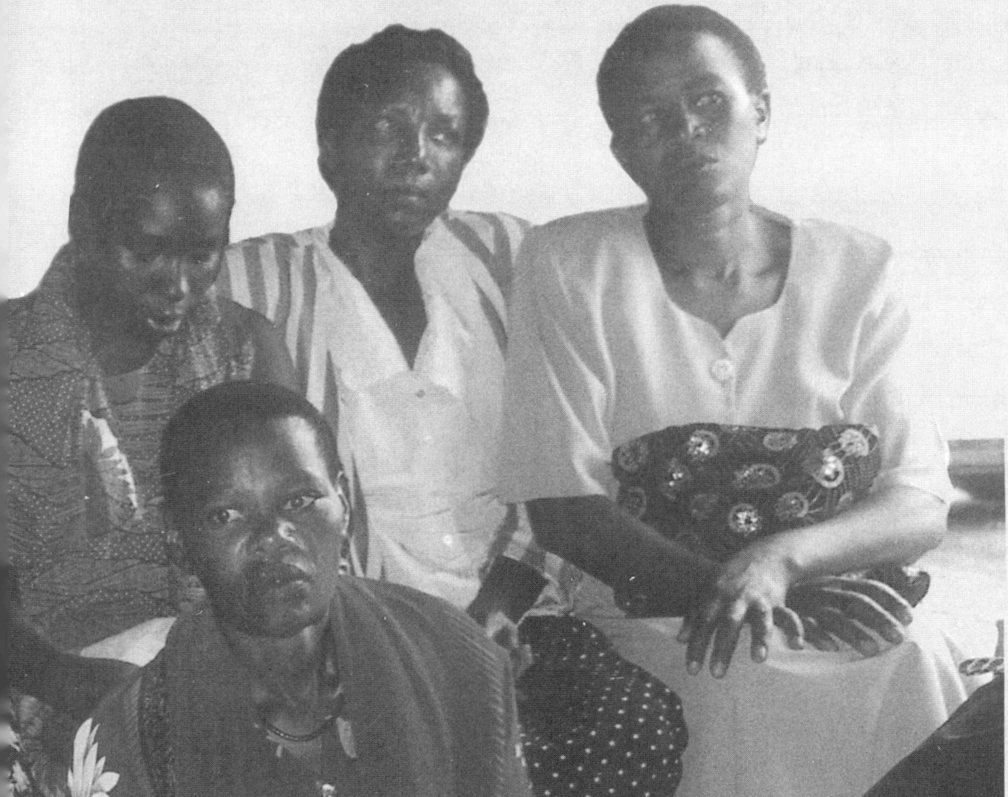

If we had co-ownership of land...

CONSTANCE NIWAGABA
Member, Bunono-Ihunga Association for Women Living with HIV and AIDS
Interview by Kaori Izumi, in Kampala, May 2002, and in Rukungiri, May 2003

My name is Constance. I am 42 years old. I live in Bunono village in Rukungiri District in Uganda. I got married in 1985. I had two children from a previous marriage. In 1993, my husband started to be ill. In 1995 he died.

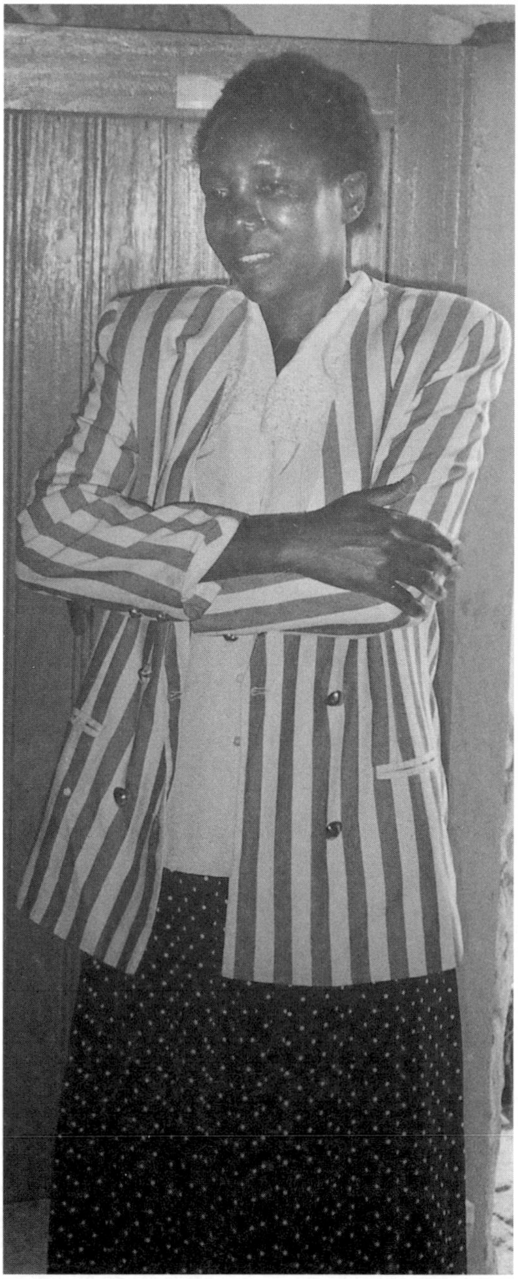

Just after my husband's death my mother-in-law and my brother-in-law started to disturb me. They threatened me that I should leave home. I reported this to the police. When I came back from the police, I found that they had taken all my belongings, including bedding, mattresses, cooking pots and plates, everything in the house, as well as my six goats.

My in-laws did not live in my village but at the place where my husband came from in Kabale District. My husband and I had moved out from our home village because of the high land pressure there. My father-in-law had bought a piece of land 10 miles away from our home village in Rukungiri District. When he died, my husband had inherited the land and lived there with his first wife, whom he then divorced before I married him. We had lived there with our children – the two children from my previous marriage and my husband's one child from his previous marriage. One of my children was in secondary school and the other in boarding primary school.

When my mother and brothers-in-law started to harass me, I left home to live with my relatives. I filed a case of theft in the magistrates' court. The magistrate told me that I should go to the local council, which I did. After the village council made a ruling that I should go back to my land, I went back home. I did not follow up the case in the magistrates' court as I found it too expensive and felt it would cause more troubles for me.

In 1997 I started to fall ill and I was admitted to a hospital for four months. When I was discharged, I had a medical bill for 140 000 Uganda shillings (US$100 in 1997). I asked to be released from the hospital and started to look for money to pay the medical bill. When I got home, I decided to sell a piece of my land to pay my medical bill. I found a buyer and sold the land and paid part of the medical bill. The piece of land I sold was fenced off by a hedge. Immediately after I had sold that piece of land, my mother-in-law and brothers-in-law came back and removed the poles from the boundary. I went to the sub-county court as the case was becoming criminal in nature. The buyer of my land had paid only half of the total price. I went to the sub-county court, which is at a higher level than village level.

I feared that my in-laws might come back to kill me. So, I rented a tiny room outside the village for nine months. Then the Administrator General of Kabale District, the district in which my in-laws live, called me because the in-laws lodged the case in Kabale District. I went to the magistrate of my sub-county and got documentation about my case. I then went to a legal officer of the Administrator General in Kabale District. I was given other documents by the magistrate at sub-county in Rukungiri District and took them to the court in Kabale four times. Finally, the judge of the High Court in Kabale dismissed the case. So, I went back to where I rented a room and stayed there for two years.

'I feared that my in-laws might come back to kill me.'

When I could no longer afford the rent, I decided to go back home to see what was happening. By then, my in-laws had stopped harassing me, and the buyer of the piece of land had made full payment. My life seemed to be getting better. But, after I had paid all the costs of travelling to all the courts, I was not able to pay off my hospital bill. I wanted to sell another piece of land to settle my medical expenses but, because of my long-standing land dispute with my in-laws, people did not want to buy my land, fearing possible trouble. I paid two-thirds of my medical bill, but I still had outstanding Ush.40 000 to pay (US$40). The full amount of the bill was Ush.100 000 (US$71).

In April 2001, the hospital took me to the local police because I had not managed to settle the bill. I was put in a prison for one night. I made a statement that I would pay the rest of the bill, but have been unable to pay because I often fall sick. Now I go only to the local clinic, not the hospital, as I still have not managed to pay off the hospital bill.

I decided to visit The AIDS Support Organisation (TASO) in Mbarara. TASO is an NGO supporting HIV and AIDS patients but their office is very far from where I live. TASO gave me an HIV and AIDS test and gave me some medicine. However, I am not able to visit them often as I cannot afford the transport costs as it is 60 miles away from my village. The travel itself costs Ush.8 000 (US$5.70), which is far beyond my capacity.

Now I am not able to grow crops on my own, and my friends and relatives come to help me. I have three acres of land and have sold 0.6 of an acre. I have a banana plantation and I also grow some other food crops. I hire labour at Ush.20 000 (US$14) per season and make payments twice per year. I sell some of the bananas to pay for the labour. My relatives pay school fees for my elder son and I pay for my younger son. My relatives help me with farming five days a week. I pay them Ush.1 000 (70 cents, US) per day for three days and they work the other two days for free. I am only able to weed the banana plantation and have to hire casual labourers to do the rest of the work. Permanent agricultural labourers cost Ush.25 000 (US$17.80) per month.

I am not able to grow enough food for my family and my relatives usually help me. If I had the money to trade, I would like to open a kiosk so that I do not need to do farming. But I continually need money for medicine.

In 1998, I started the Bunono-Ihunga Association for Women Living with HIV and AIDS, together with 20 other women from two parishes. We do some handicrafts and visit churches and schools to sensitise people about HIV and AIDS. We are also engaged in other income-generating activities, such as raising pigs and goats. I am treasurer of our association. The group now consists of 24 women and the majority of them are widows. On International AIDS Day on 1 December 2002, we performed a drama at the District Council Office on HIV and AIDS, which we had written ourselves. We acted ourselves. We would like to buy a video camera to record our performance on video.

In our association, we have a member whose husband died so she wanted to move somewhere else. She decided to sell her land, but the buyer did not pay her the full amount because her brother-in-law stopped him. She wanted to sell the land so she could buy a piece of land near her relatives. The village council decided that she should come back to her marital land and the payment the buyer had made should be returned to him. She and her two-year-old child were ill and she had already spent the money she had received for treatment. Now she is very ill. When both she and her child die, the relatives will most likely take the land.

It would be good if we as women could have co-ownership of our land with our husbands, but village councils will have difficulty in enforcing it.

Since we first formed, we have lost some of our women and new members have joined. One of our members is now representing HIV-positive people on our village council.

October 2004 (Interview by Maude Mugisha, a development consultant, Rukungiri)

I am not feeling well. I have chest pains and some cough. My body feels generally weak. I need to have a check-up.

I no longer get any money from the bananas. This is a bad season. The plantation is not weeded. I am weak and not able to work and I have no money to pay for labour. Things are really bad. I cannot even afford to travel to Rukungiri for treatment. A TASO office has been opened in Rukungiri and that is nearer than Mbarara, but I still cannot afford to go.

December 2004 (Interview by Maude Mugisha, Rukungiri)

I am now much better. I went to TASO Rukungiri as you advised me. I borrowed money and went. They examined me and gave me treatment. The chest is okay and the cough has stopped. I am feeling much better. I can now do some little work in my garden.

I am happy that my son has joined university on a government scholarship. At least I know he will complete his studies, God willing. The younger boy left school. He was too old for his class and he decided to leave. He started a small kiosk where he sells various things. He has just started and has not been able to generate any money.

People helped me and my banana plantation is now okay. I hope that I will be able to sell some bananas in January.

The Sibabinywere Women's Group, Kisasi, Ntinda, Kampala

The Sibabinywere Women's Group, Kisasi, Ntinda, Kampala was formed in 2002. The chairperson of the group, Edivina Kyoheirwe, participated in the FAO/OXFAM workshop on women's land rights in 2003, where she testified on her experiences of HIV and AIDS, domestic violence and the loss of her property.

The group had 27 members in October 2003. Before moving to Kampala, most of them were farmers in rural areas. They were chased away from family land by their in-laws when their husbands died of AIDS. Some of them were chased away because of accusations that they had bewitched their husbands and others because they came from a different tribe.

The members engaged in various economic activities, including casual labour, such as washing clothes, weeding, cleaning, working as a house girl, running a kiosk, baby-sitting and selling maize, sweet potatoes, home-made liquor and charcoal.

The group received donations worth Ush.50 000 (US$35) in 2003, of which Ush.30 000 was spent on building a shelter for the chickens. The remaining money was used to buy 25 chickens. The group also bought one pig with the donations. The group needs a sustainable project with technical management skills and financial support. In order for them to initiate any viable project, they need a location for the project and a more permanent shelter to live in.

Suffering is not dying

EDIVINA KYOHEIRWE
Chairperson, Sibabinywere Women's Group, Kisasi, Ntinda, Kampala
Interview by Kaori Izumi, Kampala, May 2002 and October 2003

My name is Edivina Kyoheirwe. I originally come from Rukungiri District and got married in Ntumgamo District. When I first got married, I was living in Kampala as a housewife. We had a piece of land in Mpigi District, just outside the city, where I was growing food. I sold produce and bought 20 pigs and 200 rabbits. I had a small shop and bought a freezer.

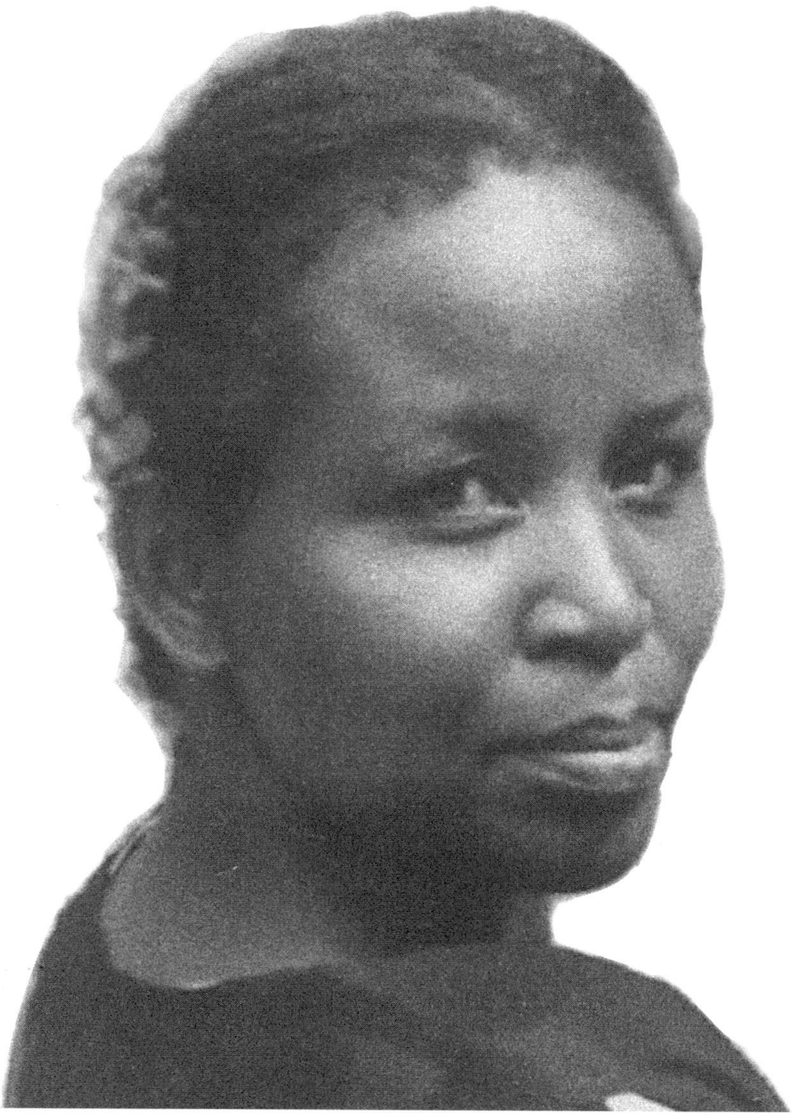

One day I found out that my husband had sold some of the pigs without consulting me. When I complained, he asked me if I thought the land belonged to me. He demanded that I should close the shop as I was getting stubborn. I closed the shop and took the freezer to my friend's house. At that time, I was not aware that my husband was ill. My husband used to work at Total and had two cars, but then he stopped working and stayed at home, while I continued working on another plot to grow food crops for sale. I was still raising pigs and rabbits.

I stopped growing food crops as my husband complained and asked me if I had come with a piece of land from my father. He told me that he was ill. He said he was going to sell everything he had because it was me who had infected him. He wanted to sell the land where I was growing food. But there was no buyer. So he sold the plot on which we were living near Kampala, without telling me. I reported this to the village court. The court told me that my husband had no right to sell the land and he should pay back the money to the buyer. However, when he paid the money back, he was angry and told me that he did not want to have anything more to do with our children. He started beating me.

One day he poured boiling sauce on the face of one of my children and he threw away our food. When the child was burnt, I took the case to the village court. My husband told the court that it was just a mistake and he had actually wanted to burn me, not our daughter. On another occasion, when I went outside to the bathroom, he was waiting for me with a big knife. The village court said that it was becoming complicated and I should go to the police. My husband told me that he was not chasing me away and I should stay with him, adding that he would kill me one day.

I went again to the police, who advised me to move out of the house. I went to my relatives with my 12-year-old son. We have two boys and two girls. My husband did not want the boys. He started beating our eldest son, who was 14 at the time, blaming him for everything. This son disappeared from home for three months. When I visited FIDA-Uganda (The Uganda Association for Women Lawyers), my husband was called. He told FIDA that he would make me suffer until I died.

My husband now lives with our two girls, who are 14 and 19 years old. He told our daughters that it was me who had infected him and he would kill me. He said that I should go back to my father's village where I have land. He refused to pay school fees for the boys, so they do not go to school anymore. My daughters are at school. My husband wrote a will, which one of my daughters has seen. The will said that his property should go to his sisters and his mistress with whom he has a daughter, and that my daughters will be given land in his village.[13] He does not want to give his land in Kampala to our sons, as he fears that if he did so, they will give the land to me when he has died.

My husband has a good pension and gets support for his treatment, while I have none. I wish my husband would die, but I do not want anything from him.

Now I have returned to live with my parents in their village and I have rented a small room near the roadside for trading. I am also keeping a room in Kampala and I stay there when I come to the city for treatment. My daughters come to visit me there. The police have told me that I should not divorce as when he dies I could claim his property as his legitimate wife.

I buy beans and maize in the villages and sell them in distant markets. It is hard for me to carry the products to the market. When I stay in Kampala, I sell tomatoes and oranges. I prefer to stay around Kampala so that I can keep contact with my children as I feel that I could still help them, even if I do not have much money. My elder daughter told me that they think they should not stay with their father.

I have met many women in Kampala who are in the same situation as me. Many of them are widows, with children, who are living with HIV and AIDS, who lost everything they had when their husbands died and had to leave their rural home and now live as squatters in Kampala. Some of them have no permanent place to stay.

In 2002, we formed a group called the Sibabinywere Women's Group Living with HIV and AIDS.[14] I am the chairperson of the group. The group has 27 members. The majority of them are widows, while a few are separated. Before moving to Kampala, most of them were farmers in rural areas. The majority of our members were chased away from their family land by their in-laws when their husbands died of AIDS. Some of us have been accused of bewitching our husbands or coming from different tribes. Two were landless and renting a piece of land for farming while their husbands were alive but were evicted when he died.

'Some of us have been accused of bewitching our husbands.'

One of our members who is a cleaner sleeps wherever she washes clothes for the day as a casual labourer. Another woman used to live in a charcoal house which collapsed. The group is helping her to rebuild the house, while her children have been dispersed to live with different friends of hers. Some of our members were evicted when their landlord found out their HIV status. A house girl also lost her job when her employer found out about her HIV status.

Depending on their experiences and the status of their health, individual members have different ideas for economic activities if some funds could be made available. These include starting a hair salon, handicrafts, selling second hand clothes and shoes, opening a restaurant, selling charcoal, opening a kiosk, sewing, selling cold drinks, etc. None of our children attend school regularly because we are not able to pay school fees. At present we are engaged in various economic activities including casual labour (washing clothes, weeding), cleaning, selling roasted maize and sweet potatoes as well as charcoal and homemade liquor-making, and baby-sitting.

When we received a donation, we built a shelter for chickens and bought 25 chicks. We have lost some of them because we were not able to buy chicken feed. Those that survived, we sold at Christmas time. If we could be resettled outside Kampala as a group, we could build a shelter for ourselves and a proper structure for rearing chickens. Then we could try to get regular buyers for them. None of us has had any experience with poultry, but we could learn and do better work if we could get some training.

One year later (Interview, October 2004, by Eric Tumwesigye, translator on visits to Rukungiri)
First of all, I still live in my funny one-roomed structure. I am currently working as a casual labourer for two people, one is a lady and she works for Hotel Equatorial and another one is a man who married recently. My duties in these two places are to wash kitchen utensils like plates, cups, saucepans etc., on a daily basis and I am paid Ush.10 000 (US$6) per month in return. There is a possibility that when the bride gets familiar, or after the honeymoon, my services may cease to be required. At the house of my female boss, I wash her clothes and iron them twice a week and she pays me Ush.8 000 (US$5.70). That is how my dear son Tomas and I have been surviving. My female boss also is mentioning shifting to another place and I may not manage to keep my job if the distance is not walkable.

I am also charged with the responsibility to supervise the group's project. We have three pigs and we are a group of 15 members. This project was formed using the donation that we received. We also received some sweaters as donations which were made by women living with HIV and AIDS in Rukungiri District. This was an attempt to see if women in Rukungiri and we could start some joint venture. We sold the sweaters and the income was used to buy three piglets. The well-wishers gave us four sweaters and we sold each of them at the price of Ush.5 000 each, except one, which we sold at Ush.15 000, but the person who bought it never paid us. We are considering suing him to the court officials. Again, we cannot forget the money that another visitor gave us. He gave us Ush.40 000 (US$30), which we used to feed our young chicks. We sold these chickens, too, and the money was part of what we used to buy three piglets.

At the moment, my life is not so worrying; I am still strong and that is why I have been able to do casual work to earn a living. However, recently I developed a terrible headache and some minor skin rashes and, after I underwent some medical examinations, the doctor told me to improve on diet and to drink a lot. He recommended drinks like yoghurt and milk. My major challenge is how to get the money to buy these drinks and good food since I earn very little money. A packet of yoghurt, for example, costs Ush.800 (50 cents, US). So how many do you think I can afford daily or on weekly basis? It is not possible for me to afford that and that means my immunity will get weaker as time goes on, but God has plans for every creature in this universe.

Personally, I have not done any projects apart from working as a casual labourer. I used to volunteer at TASO Uganda to distribute food stuff to my fellow patients, but they no longer call me and I do not know why. But I am responsible for the group's project. I also do counselling, especially to my colleagues who are faced with mental, social/psychological problems, and also planning for my future and the whole group at large. Also, let me tell you the good news that one of our three pigs delivered eight piglets and that has improved our morale, since our project has started producing good results.

Personally, I want to specialise in selling cold drinks and that has been my long plan, only that I lacked money to begin with. If I get a fridge and some starting capital, I will start. I have saved Ush.20 000 so far and when we sell our piglets as a group we want to share the money amongst ourselves and invest it in individual projects. This is because we cannot afford to keep these piglets for more than three months because we do not have enough land. If we are to maintain them, we need a big land where to dig some foods for these pigs, build a bigger structure, etc. Therefore, I anticipate sharing Ush.40 000, which will increase my savings from Ush.20 000 to Ush.60 000 (US$ 14–43). I have plans to buy a second-hand fridge for Ush.250 000 (US$178.50) and to save some starting capital.

I need one or two crates of sodas, a small Brenda machine, some money to buy passion fruits and a few other things to use for boiling and keep water in the fridge. I need to work hard to increase my savings in order to begin my own business. This will enable me to provide some basic needs for my children who are still living by the mercy of good Samaritans. One of them is paying school fees for my son Tomas and has always contributed money to buy things like books and knickers for my children at the beginning of every term when they are planning to go to school. The fact that three of my children are staying with their father is not enough to mean that their living conditions are good. They have always asked me for the basic needs, which their father is not willing to provide, and for the girls especially they need to be given extra care. Things like pads and knickers are very important, the books and pocket money is also necessary, but their father regards some of these as minor requirements and yet they are important for young students to have. I am struggling to provide the very urgent ones so that my girls do not resort to bad acts in order to meet their needs.

I feel that one day things will change and I will live a better life before I leave this world. There is a saying, 'Okubonabona Sikufa', meaning that 'suffering is not dying'.

We are 15 active and devoted members. Initially we were 28 registered members but some of our colleagues left or deserted the group. As a group of 15 members, we have three pigs and eight piglets, as earlier mentioned. The other two are also expecting and I believe our project is not doing so badly. We shall keep on selling the young ones after two to three months of maturity and share the money to boost individual projects.

We believe that if we get enough land our group project will expand and we shall construct some structure to keep both chicken broilers and layers. We could also build a house for our pigs, which will be big enough to keep more than three pigs. On the same land, if acquired, we are planning to construct an office and a house for the person who will be keeping or looking after our project. I, on behalf of the members of the group, hope that our supporters can assist us in having a meaningful future. That's all I can say.

HIV has given me a longer and more meaningful life

Surviving domestic violence, property-grabbing, and HIV and AIDS

FLAVIA KYOMUKAMA

Ugandan VSO volunteer and co-ordinator of a UNESCO youth programme on communication on HIV and AIDS in Mozambique, 2005

First presented at a national workshop on 'HIV and AIDS, and Women's Property Rights and Livelihoods in Zimbabwe', Harare, Zimbabwe, 1–2 December 2004

Many of us here have faced stigma and discrimination of different kinds. It could have been work, family, community or medical. My specific discrimination and ostracism was from my immediate family. I was stripped of all property, my academic documents destroyed and I was denied access to my three children.

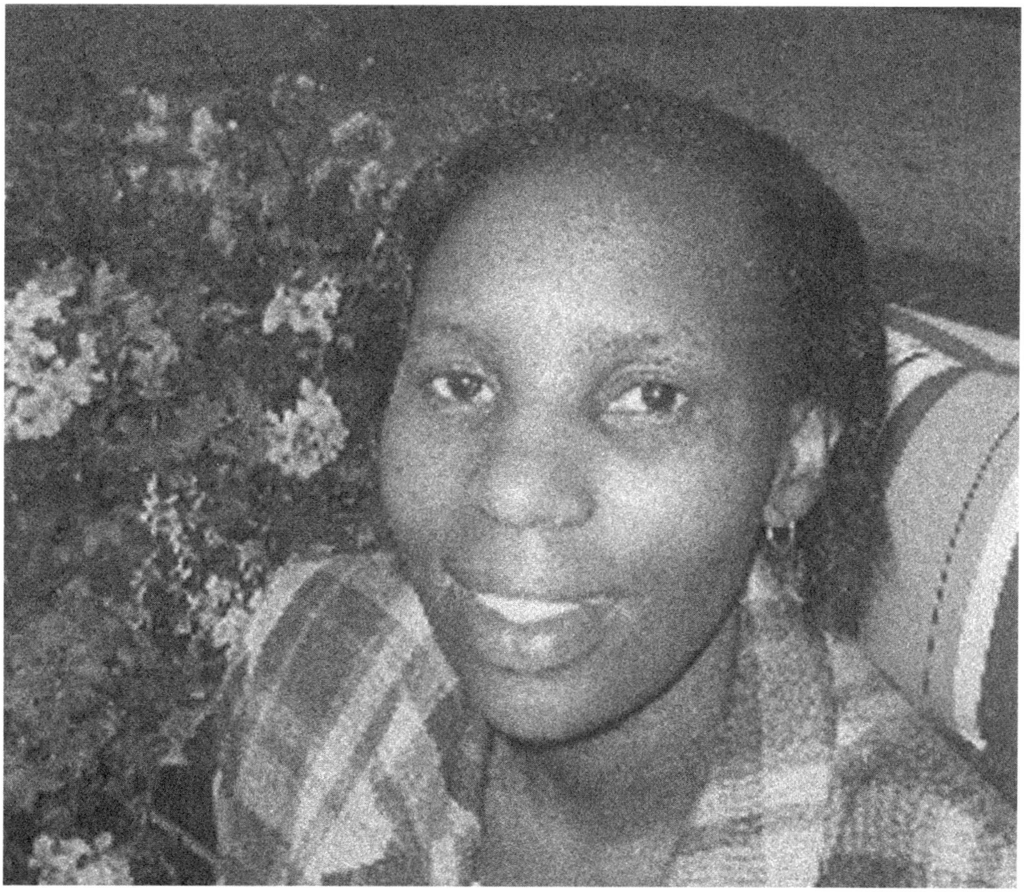

The gist of the matter is that I married at the age of 19 when I had just finished high school. If I had been older, maybe things would have been different. I met this university graduate who seemed very enterprising and we embarked on family formation. We did not test for HIV because then it was little known and little information was available in Uganda in 1989. I graduated as a secondary school teacher in 1991 and I started teaching in a government-aided school.

I lost my first delivery – twins – and the third-born also died. In 1994 I developed TB, was tested and found to be HIV-positive. My husband was also tested positive soon after. We agreed to live positively. But as time went on he started battering me, trying to alienate me from family and friends. He did not want me to get any additional employment, do any kind of paid work or job to boost my pay. He was not giving me what I needed and on the government payroll, I was not earning much. Whenever I tried, he would ask me to choose between him and the potential job. Of course I would leave that aside in the interest of family cohesion and the sake of the children.

Having married at this tender age, of course, as our culture demands, I continued with my job of procreation. I produced two other children but, for the last one, I managed to have the Prevention of Mother to Child Transmission Therapy (PMTCT). After this delivery in 1999, I stayed home to care for my child, for I was not meant to breastfeed if I was to protect her from infection. I then lost my high-school teaching job. I now became penniless; he would not leave me any money, he would do the entire shopping, cut off the fixed telephone at home so I had no communication with the outside, etc.

In the year 2000, he started complaining that I was eating for nothing and that I should get a job. I tried but it was hard. If I went to town to seek for a job, he would say I was just gossiping around. I was dumbfounded. I didn't know what to do.

Luckily enough there was advertising for a master's programme at the university. I applied and was admitted. When I asked him to pay the tuition for me he said it was my problem. I asked because for all the 12 years, between 1989 and 2001, when I had been with him, we had accumulated property and I knew profit from these assets would cover my fees. But he refused. My brothers, sisters and my parents agreed to contribute for me to do the course and this time hell broke lose. He was not amused. He would ask how these people could pay for me when my husband did not. He took me to the police and told them I would die of HIV if I went for this course. He was told the contrary – that I would live longer if I was kept busy. He did not like that either. He called elders and friends, only to be advised to respect my decision and to support me.

He became more violent and I left him for about a month in 2000. He came after me and of course, as a mother, I went back for the children's sake. Little did I know that sticking with the marriage could have cost me my life. He somehow came to terms with my education course, but he was abusive and I stood it. He could humiliate me before my children, employees and in public. He would shout at me, chase me from the house at night and isolate me. I still can't imagine that I went through all that.

During my first year of the course I could get research work, but he would lock me in the house so I couldn't earn. When I completed my first year in 2001, his father called me to the village, which was my marital village. I found people had gathered; I was alone with his clan leaders and also him. He declared he did not want me any longer. He drove me and left me at the roadside about 60 km from my home at 5 pm on that Saturday. It was raining. Luckily I reached my parent's home at about 10 o'clock with my suitcase, which my husband gave me as all that belonged to me after 12 years. He took everything, even my academic qualifications he destroyed, but that was dumb of him because the university is still functioning.

He denied me access to my 2-year-old, 7-year-old and 11-year-old and planted guards at the house, the very house at which I laid the first brick for construction. (Recently I learnt that these guards who kept me away all died of AIDS early this year.) I tried to appeal to court for custody of my two younger children. The case dragged on until 2003. It was so frustrating and draining all my energy and my CD 4 cell-count dropped drastically. I withdrew and gave the children to God.

'I can use my lesson to save a life.'

However, before he chased me away, he had changed ownership of our assets to himself, his mother and my two elder boys (7 and 11 years old). My daughter and I were left out and stripped of our property. This was partly the reason I went back for a second degree, I wanted something I could own alone and have full security of. My 12 years of energy had been so abused.

On the other side, I thanked him for chasing me away because if I had remained there with all the stress, coupled with HIV and AIDS, I would be dead by now. I managed to get jobs immediately after he chased me. I joined several organisations, for example, the National Community of Women Living with HIV and AIDS, the AIDS Information Centre and the church choir. I accepted my life and resolved not to die for the man who mistreated me, and then I asked God for three years more so I could prove myself. He did, and now I have asked for longer life till old age. I have been blessed with job opportunities because I am always hardworking, and today I am able to volunteer in Mozambique for the UNESCO/UNFIP project on HIV and AIDS communication among the youth. I have changed many people's lives with my testimony and I hope to help others to not fall into the pit that I landed in.

However, this was a good experience and a lesson to me and God did this for a purpose. I can use my lesson to save a life. My children are with him but they will come back one day. I am not worried, for one good thing about him is that he actually loves them. I am not a widow as many of us are here but many widows are in a better situation than me; what I went through was too bad. However, it gave me a future. I am able to get free ARVs from the DART Programme for the next four years, till 2008, and I am assured of a longer life if I take the pills prescribed. 'If God is for me who can be against me?' as the saying goes.

We are here to stay. Let's not rush to die; let's join hands and fight for our future. HIV and AIDS is manageable, preventable, let's just spread the gospel. These cultures that abuse us will soon be no more if we send our daughters to school and they are equipped with skills to manage their lives. The biggest gift my mother ever gave me, besides bearing me, was education. I wonder where and how I would be, if I had been illiterate; probably dead by now.

In our African culture we are blessed with the gift of extended family attachment. Let's continue to use this setting. In my case, my family, friends and peers supported me until the time I was reintegrated into ordinary life with less threats and abuse.

As we commemorate World AIDS Day 'HIV and AIDS, women and girls', we should remember that it's never too late; we are in this as women together – for a positive difference. If I survived it, why not others? HIV and AIDS are generous; many times it gives us time to self reflect on our lives for a better future. We must continue to educate the world and be role models in all our endeavours; use our experiences to empower and strengthen those in need of our support and care.

We all have unique skills. We should not refrain from using them for the betterment of our fellow kith and kin – the womenfolk.

For God and our lives, for health is in our hands, let's make the best out of it now.

Thanks for enabling me to attend this workshop and more thanks to the organisers, who feel with us and are willing to fight for us in this cause.

The Memory Book Project

The Memory Book includes training for both parents and guardians and children or dependent children. It is a very useful way of giving children up to date and real life information for their own benefit. They are trained or given life skills to prevent HIV infection and to care and support their parents when sick. The children learn to be empathetic at the right time in their life and may even start planning their future early. They get ready to take on life based on the information and life skills they acquire in the Memory Book training.

Planning for the future

The Memory Book Project is a family project for guardian and foster children or parents and biological children. It is a simple means of keeping families and their assets together and therefore assuring dependants of sustainable livelihoods in the future. This project teaches the basics about parenting, communication skills (to parents and children as well as guardians and foster children), the disclosure of HIV status by parents to children and children to parents, preparing for eventual separation of families in the event of death, and how parents and children can handle death when it comes. In the last section, the Memory Book offers planning for the future, which involves parents making wills and therefore securing the children's property in the future. In fact, it is a simple way of showing family and children the facts about their property before parents die. It is a simple way of ensuring children are not stripped of property, since it does not upset anyone's expectations, unlike presenting a will for the first time to people who expect to be beneficiaries.

New relationships

In parenting skills, the training analyses involvement in new relationships after the death of a spouse by the surviving spouse. Many infected mothers are still young and able to get into long relationships again. This training makes them aware of possible exploitation by the other sex, especially when the widow has property. Many people have remarried and ended up unhappy; for instance, the new spouse abuses the children sexually, physically and psychologically. So surviving mothers and fathers are sensitised to the need for love and affection, but taught to be careful about their choices in the interest of their own and their children's welfare.

The Memory Project training is holistic in nature, for it addresses issues of psychosocial, economic and emotional well-being. Parents need it. It is not a preserve for persons living with HIV but for all parents, especially where there is a flaw in communication. Despite its tragic effect, HIV and AIDS has been a blessing in disguise to society, for it is reawakening the need for societies and families to plan together their future livelihoods.

Flavia Kyomukama, March 2005

Liberated from secrecy, accountable to our children

BEATRICE WERE

Founder, Memory Book Project and Team Leader HIV and AIDS, Sexual and Reproductive Rights, Health, Policy and Advocacy, Action Aid International, based in Uganda.

Interview by Kaori Izumi, March 2005

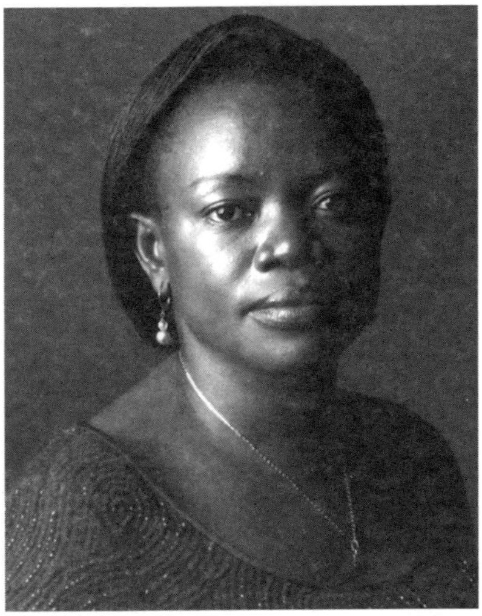

As a woman living with HIV, the biggest challenge for me was how to open up my status to my own children. I was tested positive and disclosed my HIV status in public in 1995, but without telling my children. I had a high sense of guilt to my children. I had told everybody in big conferences, including UN conferences. The fact that I had not told my children was the biggest burden in my life at that time. I felt that I should be more accountable to my children than to anybody else. Other HIV-positive women were also in the same situation. While all of us thought it was important to disclose to our children, we did not know how to do it or when the right time was. I started to draft a concept document on what to say and how to deal with reactions from children when their mothers have disclosed. I discussed the idea with some of the international donors, but they felt it was difficult and not feasible to implement.

Then I met a woman from the UK, Carol Lindsay-Smith, who was a retired social worker. As a social worker, she had worked with children, including those from African communities living in the UK. She was visiting Uganda. I shared my nightmare with her. When I died, how would my children best deal with stigma, etc.? I was writing a small note on it. Carol had worked with children with parents dying of cancer in the UK. Some were black patients from Africa who wanted to prepare their children for when their parents died abroad. Carol showed me a book which contained documentation on the life history of the parents to help children prepare for the death of their parents.

I started drafting a broader concept, adapting this book to the Ugandan context and HIV and AIDS. What remained was how to talk to children and the effect of disclosure on the children. I felt that the book should be not frightening and be a part of a broader project. My concept included issues such as:

- Giving mothers skills to communicate with children on what they will go through after parents have disclosed;
- Dealing with the stigma of HIV and AIDS;

- Collecting important family information on original homes and close relatives, property and inheritance, and important valuables (such as photos to remember the parents by) which mean a lot to children.

When parents are still alive, they need to use the time for the benefit of their children by securing plans for their children. This includes making a will to safeguard property and starting to guide children on guardians who will look after them, foster parents, etc. Children need to be involved in important decisions which will affect them, such as what to do with the home, school arrangements, and relationships with guardians/foster parents, etc. It is important to put children at the centre of decision-making. We need to answer the questions asked by our children while we are still alive and guide them on how to deal with them.

'The Memory Book has done something tremendous to my life.'

I organised a group of women living with HIV and tried out my concept. Some international organisations showed interest and we tried the idea in Kampala as a pilot. By 2000, most of the large international aid organisations involved with HIV and children had picked up the idea of the Memory Book. It has been introduced in Kenya, Zimbabwe, Tanzania and South Africa, as far as I know.

The Memory Book has done something tremendous to my life. I have overcome the burden of secrecy. Before, I could not take medicine in front of my children because I was afraid that they would ask me questions. The Memory Book liberated me from this burden. It was such a liberating experience in my life.

Since I conceived the initial idea of the Memory Book in 1996, a lot of changes have happened around HIV and AIDS. New drugs were found and parents live longer than before. There is a need to incorporate these new messages into the Memory Book Project.

Country profile **Zambia**

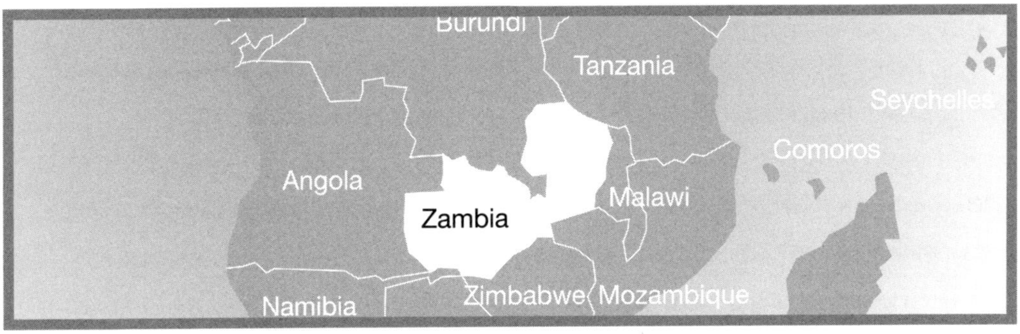

At independence in 1964, Zambia inherited a strong mining-based economy, which deteriorated in the mid-1970s following a sharp decline in copper prices (FAO 2003e). The population of Zambia was estimated to be 11.3 million in 2003 and life expectancy is 37.5 years (UNDP 2005). Almost half of the total population is urban-based. The share of agriculture in the GDP averaged 18 per cent over the past decade, with a GDP per capita of US$ 417 (UNDP 2005). Agriculture provides a livelihood for about 60 per cent of the population and employment for about 67 per cent of the total labour force (FAO 2003e). It is the main source of income and employment for women. About 70 per cent of the population is currently estimated to live below the poverty line.

The spread of HIV and AIDS has a significant impact on the food and agriculture economy, in both the short and long term. It is estimated that 920 000 adults and children are living with HIV and AIDS (UNAIDS 2004). The total number of adult women who are living with HIV is 470 000 and approximately 85 000 children are living with the disease (UNAIDS 2004). By 2003, 89 000 people had died of AIDS, resulting in 630 000 orphans. HIV prevalence in young pregnant women in Lusaka, the capital city, was estimated to be 22.1 per cent in 2002. The recent spread of AIDS has created a new and growing class of impoverished widows and orphans. This has increased the vulnerability of the female and child populations, exposing them to poverty and food insecurity. The GDP per capita for females is almost half of what it is for men: $554, compared to $1,009 (UNDP 2005).

While 12 per cent of Zambia's landmass is suitable for arable use, only about 14 per cent of that arable land is presently cultivated (FAO 2003e). Approximately 92 per cent of the land is under a customary land tenure system, as opposed to 6 per cent for freehold/leasehold land. The Land Act of 1995 made it possible for local communities on customary land, after consultation with and the consent of traditional chiefs, to obtain title to land. The impact of this situation on the land rights of women is an area that needs further analysis.

The Intestate Succession Act of 1989 was introduced to end property-grabbing in cases where a deceased spouse has not left a written will (COHRE 2004). The Act, as reformed in 1996, provides for inheritance rights of multiple wives. By law, the spouse is to have a life interest in the house, which 'shall terminate upon that spouse's remarriage', and it is illegal to evict a surviving spouse from the matrimonial home. The earlier resentment at the passing of the law, which usurped customary rights, had blossomed into a blatant disregard of statutory law and a perpetuation of the distorted and cruel practice of property-grabbing. The law is weakened, first and foremost, by the lack of conviction among women themselves that they have a legal right to their deceased husband's property. The 1995 Land Act is formally gender-neutral and women can apply for title to land. However, the Act also allows for the customary laws of an area to be paramount and women's applications for land have been rejected as contrary to customary law (WLSA 2001). In 1999, the Ministry of Lands made a policy announcement that 10 per cent of all advertised plots of land should be allocated to women (Walker 2002).

The Justice for Widows and Orphans Project (JWOP)

The project was formed in 2001 as a result of a study on the plight of widows and orphans in Zambia, which was commissioned by the Embassy of Finland. The study revealed the suffering of widows and orphans and recommended the formation of a project to uplift the legal status of widows and orphans in Zambia. The JWOP is a non-governmental organisation established to sensitise widows and orphans on their basic human rights, advocate for legal reform, and promote and safeguard the rights of widows and orphans in Zambia. The project started operating in March 2001, bringing together seven organisations to form a network.

The overall objective of the organisation is to strive to advocate, promote and safeguard the rights of all citizens, especially widows and orphans in Zambia. This mission relates to improving awareness about the institutional and legal provisions concerning the status of widows and orphans in Zambia. Among those to be targeted in awareness campaigns are the community leaders, such as chiefs and headpersons, government officials, and functionaries responsible for enacting and enforcing laws.

The activities of the organisation include:

- Advocating for laws and policies that promote justice for widows and orphans;
- Forming widows' support groups;
- Training widows in inheritance laws and providing paralegal advice;
- Broadcasting general sensitisation programmes on community radio and national television;
- Documenting cases studies and establishing a resource base;
- Addressing the consequences of HIV and AIDS through counselling, survival-skills training and referral for treatment.

The JWOP is working directly with widows and orphans who have been victims of discriminatory laws and practices relating to land rights and inheritance.

I am a widow living with 16 graves

THERESA CHILALA[15]

Monze, Zambia

Interview by Florence Shakafuswa, Lusaka, January 2005

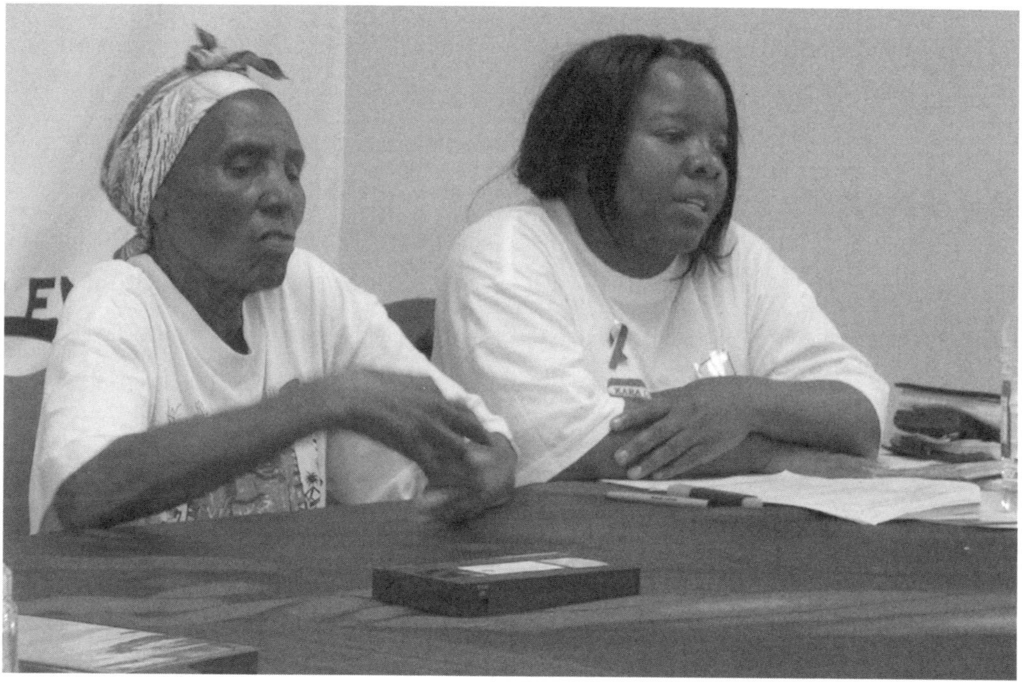

I got married at 17 years old to my husband, who was a teacher. My husband was from the royal family of headmen and he got some land in the area where we settled. My father-in-law was a polygamist, and so he had other children from his other wife. I had some problems with the other family of my husband. When we moved to the land we wanted to settle on, the other family also moved and we had quarrels over land for grazing of our animals. The other family kept on pushing their boundary nearer our land and their animals started coming into our fields for grazing. This caused tension between the two families.

Since my husband was a teacher, he was transferred to work in the districts and so we moved. Finally, we went back home when he retired. However, the squabbles with the other family did not end. My husband decided to shift to a new area but even there the other family claimed part of the land. The quarrels started again. The new land we moved to was land where my husband's father was buried in 1939. This was the only grave that we found there. My husband died in 1990, a few months after we had shifted to the new land. This is when problems with my husband's half-brother persisted.

After funeral rites were performed, one of my husband's real brothers collected everything from the house. This included all the oxen, ploughs and household goods. By our village standards, my family was well off, since my husband had been working in the government and we had reasonably good furniture and over 30 cows. The iron-roofing sheets of my house were also taken. Usually, village houses have grass roofs, so my in-laws were very happy to have acquired iron sheets.

My husband's half-brother wanted to inherit me but I refused. I also recall that some time when I was still with my husband he made advances towards me but I had refused then. This aggravated my situation, as he wanted to punish me for refusing his proposal. Besides, my children were still willing to continue staying on the land and so I decided to stay there also. In 1994, he buried his brother on my land. I went to the headman and the chief, but since they were all my brother-in-law's relatives, they did not help me. The graveyard started expanding as seven more bodies were buried there. This site is just adjacent to my house. When I saw that the local traditional leaders were not assisting the situation, I approached a local NGO, which referred me to legal-aid organisations. This NGO gave us a lawyer and my son was assisting me in the court case. The lawyers successfully put up an injunction restraining my brother-in-law from further burials.

'We heard a lot of terrifying stories from orphans and widows.'

We used to go to court from time to time. I was asked to stay in our capital city because I could not afford transport money to travel every time the case was in court. The case started while the previous government was in power. When the new president came into power, new judges were appointed. I did not hear from the court until I was served with the judgement. In effect, the courts were saying that they had no jurisdiction over the case and referred me back to the chief. I now owe my brother-in-law 50 million Kwacha (US$12 000) for his legal costs. Since the judgement, my brother-in-law has continued to bury his relatives on our land. As of now there are sixteen graves.

I am so tormented and upset at the sight of the graves. I do not understand why I have to buy those graves at 50 million Kwacha. I am now 78 years old. The graves were meant to scare me from my land. I also lament how my younger children have been disturbed. One of my sons who is now a soldier used to say, when he was still very young, that what happened was very sad. He remembers handing over household goods to his uncle and quarrelling over land and burial. He says he does not find peace in going to see his mother in his village and that he does not have a home to settle in after he retires from the government.

Six months later

The 17th body was buried in front of Theresa's house on 6 June 2005.

Recovering grabbed property
The Victim Support Unit (VSU), Zambia

PETER KANUNKA
Superintendent and Director, VSU, Zambia
Presented at a national workshop on 'HIV and AIDS, and Women's Property Rights and Livelihoods in Zimbabwe', Harare, Zimbabwe, 1–2 December 2004

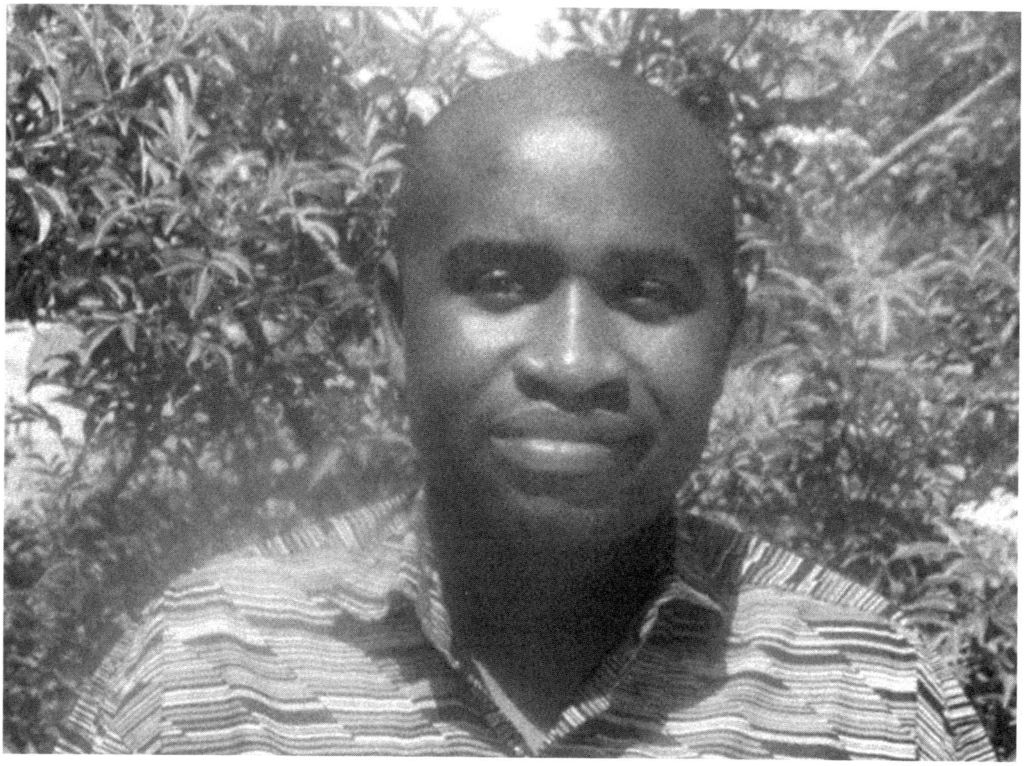

The Zambia Police Service, in its effort to combat crime at all levels, has come up with a lot of interventions. Crime in Zambia is of great concern, due to the devastating effects it has on the economy and the general welfare of the citizens. The Zambia Police Service Reform Programme of 1994 saw the birth of the VSU. The unit was legalised through the Police Amendment Act No. 14 of 1999. The main purpose of the Unit is to deal with acts of violence against women, children and the elderly. These acts were previously perceived as domestic cases. It is evident that society at large is beginning to appreciate that such acts are a violation of human rights and amount to offences against the law and, above all, undermine the rule of good governance. The main objectives of the VSU are to prevent crimes of domestic violence, sexual offences and crimes against children and elderly persons. Restoration of grabbed properties is also one of our major mandates.

A number of initiatives have been taken to respond to crimes such as spouse battery, child defilement, property-grabbing, etc. The levels of occurrence of these crimes still remain regrettably high. While the cases that are reported to the police are increasingly receiving improved attention, it is still a fact that the general response should be improved. This can be achieved through sensitisation of the community and the training of more officers in aspects of gender, human rights, psychosocial counselling, legal intervention, investigation, and so on.

The HIV and AIDS pandemic among the population has to a large extent exposed many women and children to acts of victimisation. It is a common practice among various Zambian tribes to deprive widows and orphans of their share in the estates of the deceased husbands and fathers. To some extent, widows have been subjected to sexual cleansing, the perpetrators thus hoping to be given some share of the late husband's estates, but putting the widows at risk of contracting the disease. In the event of both parents dying of HIV and AIDS and leaving orphans, the current scenario does not guarantee much property security for the children. The extended family system, which previously played a key role in such circumstances, is increasingly diminishing, as evidenced by the high number of children on the streets. It is therefore apparent that society and the police should step in to address issues of property security for orphaned children and surviving spouses.

Awareness of the plight of surviving spouses and orphans, as well as of the law affecting them, is necessary to ensure their rights are protected. Increased awareness will lead to increased reporting of cases of victimisation and human rights abuses. It is worth noting that crimes and violence against women and children have reached epidemic proportions and people need to be made aware of this.

Convictions in cases of property-grabbing have increased during the last few years. In 2001, 909 cases of property-grabbing were reported, with only 57 convictions. In 2002, 641 cases were reported and 96 convictions were made, and, in 2003, 734 reported cases led to 228 convictions being made. However, the conviction rate remains very low because widows and orphans are ignorant of the provisions of the law. They fear breaking family ties and victimisation by in-laws. Victims often opt to reconcile with their abusers. Cultural barriers, lack of access to information and resources to pursue cases and inaccessibility of services are some of the key constraints.

In order to stop widows and orphans suffering from property-grabbing there is a need to create a comprehensive response. This can be achieved through legal intervention, crisis control via support groups, the establishment and strengthening of the VSU and by sensitisation of communities through music concerts, radio and television programmes, rallies and drama performances.

Sensitisation for traditional leaders, church leaders and schools needs to be conducted. There is a need for laws to be tightened and the will-writing programme should be expanded. Consideration should be given for widows to be administrators of property. People need to be encouraged to report cases, and networking should be promoted. Widows and orphans also need support for their economic empowerment.

'Crimes and violence against women and children have reached epidemic proportions.'

Whereas the rate of conviction for property-grabbing is increasing, the number of cases reported is just the tip of the iceberg. We need to make much more effort to sensitise widows, orphans and communities on the issue of property-grabbing. The capacity of our unit needs to be strengthened through improved financial resources and technical expertise.

Country profile **Zimbabwe**

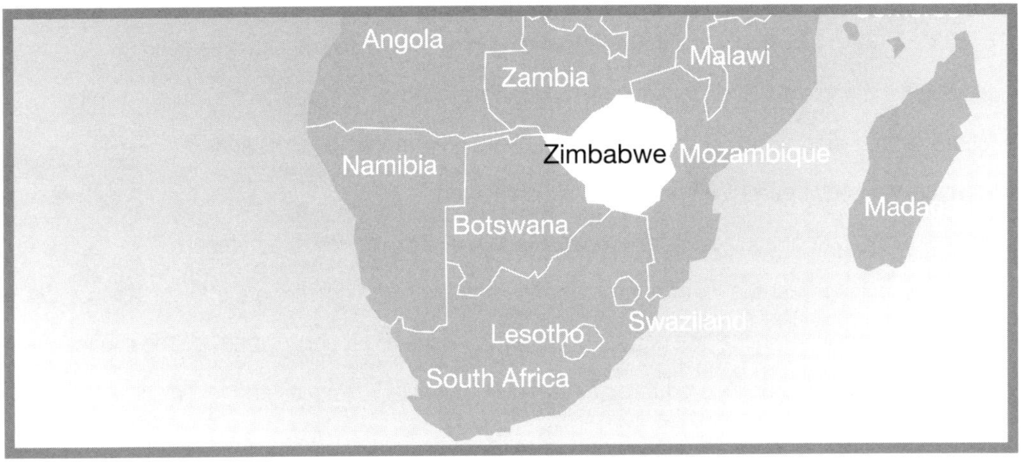

Zimbabwe is a landlocked country in southern Africa with a population of 12.9 million (UNDP 2005). Almost 70 per cent of the population is resident in the rural areas and largely depend on agriculture for its livelihood. Agriculture in Zimbabwe accounts for 17 per cent of the GDP (FAO 2005c), and about 60 per cent of the economically active population depends on this sector for employment. Women play an important role in agriculture and it is estimated that 70 per cent of small-scale farmers are women (FAO 2005c). The country has suffered from food shortages during the past few years, partly due to repeated drought conditions.

In Zimbabwe, around 1.8 million adults and children are living with HIV, including 930 000 adult women and 120 000 children. By 2003, 170 000 people had died of AIDS and 980 000 children had been orphaned due to the disease. The rate of HIV infection was estimated to be 24.8 per cent in 2003. The negative impact of HIV and AIDS in agriculture and food security is a great concern. The HIV infection rate is particularly high among farm workers on commercial farms (UNDP 2003).

Since the attainment of political independence in 1980, Zimbabwe has been implementing land reforms aimed at redressing the injustices of land distribution under colonial rule. In 2000, the Zimbabwean government launched a Fast Track Resettlement Programme. This compulsorily acquired large-scale commercial farms for resettlement. As a consequence, the land-ownership structure and the balance between white-dominated, large-scale agriculture and small-scale, black agriculture has drastically changed.

Zimbabwe's land policy encourages joint registration of land between husband and wife, although this is not mandatory. Customary law, in essence, grants land rights to adult males. In 1997, the face of Zimbabwean inheritance was radically changed, when the vitally important Administration of Estates Amendment repealed provisions of the prior Administration of Estates Act (COHRE 2004). The 1997 Amendment was aimed at giving women in customary marriage, whether registered or not, the right to inherit from their husbands. If the deceased died after November 1997, then the surviving spouse is automatically entitled to ownership of the matrimonial home. In addition to the home, the value of the estate is divided by the number of children, plus the surviving spouse (COHRE 2004). However, in 1999 the Supreme Court of Zimbabwe prevented a woman from inheriting her father's property, on the grounds that customary law dictated the property may only go to a male. This represented a major setback for women's property rights in Zimbabwe (Dodo 2003).

In May 2005, Operation *Murambatsvina* (Operation Clean Up) – intended to destroy 'illegal' vending sites, structures and other informal business premises and homes – was established (Tibaijuka 2005). This operation affected, among others, widows, single mothers and orphan-headed households who lived in illegal settlements or rented housing and who relied for their livelihoods on street vending.

Grave exhumed, house demolished, granary burnt

MARVIS HADZIUCHERI

Widow

Interviews by Bella Matambanadzo, November 2004, and Kaori Izumi, September 2005

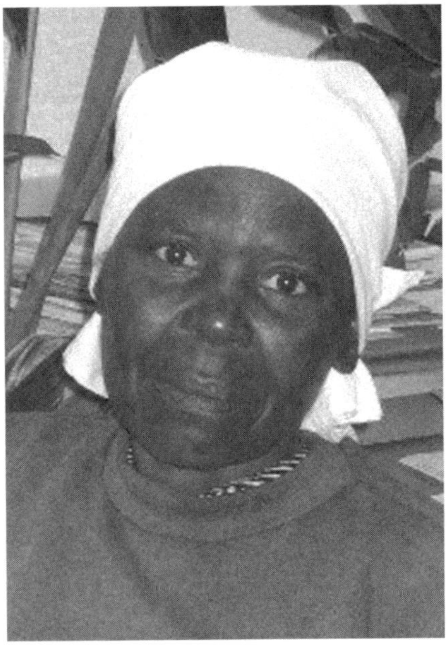

My husband died in 2004. I had been married for 28 years. My husband and I had no children. We had moved from our home in Harare to the rural areas so that I could farm more easily and more profitably on a larger plot of land which we had secured. So when my husband died, I was alone.

I sent a message to his family that he had died and they should come to bury him, but I did not hear anything from them. I sent another message without any response. After five days, I finally consulted our headman about what I should do. The headman advised me that I should go ahead with the funeral and burial. I followed his advice. Then my troubles started. Three weeks after I had already buried him, his family, my in-laws, drove 300 km south-west of the capital, Harare, to my home in rural cotton-farming Gokwe. They dug up his body, took it to my home in Harare and left it in one of the rooms until it started to decompose. They finally took it to a secret location for re-burial. I do not know where he was buried.

A few weeks later they came back again and took my household property and harvest. My home has been completely destroyed. There is nothing left: no cows, dishes, plates, not even my clothes. Nothing. They smashed down all the doors, demolished my house, burned my granary, took the crops I had harvested, farming inputs, my cows and scotch cart; all of which I had bought with the income I made from farming.

His relatives said that I had behaved as if my husband did not have family. I went to the headman to ask him for a letter so that I could get a death certificate for my husband and reclaim my property from the in-laws. The headman said he had given it to my in-laws. I found out that my in-laws had given the headman some of my cows. I went to the police, but they told me that the property belonged to the relatives and they had the right to take them. I was at a loss. I did not know what to do.

I also discovered that my husband had been married to his half-sister. I have a copy of the marriage certificate. They got a civil marriage in order to qualify for allocation to a house in Harare, because an application for housing requires a marriage certificate. My husband and his sister had different names because their fathers were different, so the city council did not realise that they were half-siblings. They were able to have the false marriage registered. My sister-in-law was saying she was my husband's widow.

My husband's marriage to his second wife was a customary marriage. But this marriage did not work out well, and finally they divorced according to the Shona tradition of *gupuro*. *Gupuro* is a ritual where the husband returns his wife to her natal home with a 20 cent coin, which means the marriage is formally over. He did return the second wife and she got remarried to somebody else and had two children with him. This second wife of my husband's was also making claims to my urban estate, saying that although divorced, she was the rightful heir. My deceased husband's relatives looked for this second wife, because they wanted to use her to take my urban estate. The first wife who was his half-sister, the second wife, and other relatives, took all my movable properties and moved into my house in Harare. I was thrown out and have been living in a broken minibus without windows, becoming a destitute.

'I will fight until I get the last penny back..'

All I want is for them to put me back in my house. I left the house with just the clothes I was wearing and I have nothing else. I will fight until I get the last penny back.

Seven months later in June 2005

I sued that case in the civil court. The court case was about who was the legitimate surviving spouse of my husband. It became clear to everyone that the second wife came back only with the interest to inherit the deceased's property, because she left him over 28 years ago and had never come back to visit him, even when he was ill. I was assisted by the Zimbabwe Widows and Orphans Trust (ZWOT) to pursue the court case. The court ruled that I was the legitimate surviving spouse, and I won the case in June 2005.

Immediately after I got the judgement, the Chaplin at Harare Central Police was contacted and asked to send a police officer who could escort me to get me back to my house in Harare. Two days after the judgement, my in-laws and fake wives were thrown out of the house and I was back in my house. Three weeks later, the second wife appealed the case, and my case is not yet over.

Recovering my property, recovering my life

RUDO CHIWANDIRE

Widow

Presented at a national workshop on 'HIV and AIDS, and Women's Property Rights and Livelihoods in Zimbabwe', Harare, Zimbabwe, 1–2 December 2004

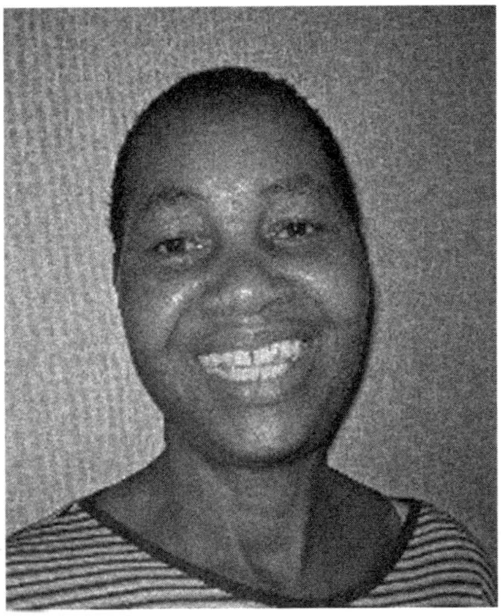

My name is Rudo Chiwandire and I am 52 years old. I was married to the late Oliver Chiwandire in 1979 and we were married under Chapter 37.[16] We were married and were blessed with four children – two boys and two girls. We lived together for 20 years, after which he died on 5 November 1999. My late husband began to show signs of not being well, he used to send one of our children to buy painkiller tablets because he had constant headaches. One day he said to me, 'My wife, I think I should resign and get all my benefits and enjoy them while I am still alive.' There was no time after he told us he was not well. In October, he collapsed and we took him to Waterfalls Nursing Home. He spent two weeks there and then he died of meningitis.

My husband's family immediately decided to sell our three-ton truck because there was no money. They sold it for Z$20 000 (US$400) only, and then they went on to share the money amongst all my husband's children. He had five children with his first wife, whom he divorced, and we had four children together. The same relatives wanted to sell our home and they did not worry where we were going to live. They did not care about my state of health.

After my husband died, his relatives wanted to take everything from our home and wanted me to go back to my father. I went to see our doctor and he showed me all my husband's medical records and that he had died of AIDS. I began to feel ill. He sent me to Wilkins for HIV tests and they found me positive. A friend of mine came to see me and shared a secret and told me to go to the Zimbabwe Widows and Orphans Trust (ZWOT): 'They will help you with all your problems.' When I went there, they helped me to register my late husband's estate with the High Court. They helped me to administer the estate until I was given the Certificate of Authority. I went on to explain how my life was and how my relatives terrorise me from time to time. The High Court gave me consent to sell and buy another house to avoid their interference.

The Zimbabwe Widows and Orphans Trust sent me to the Development Anti-Retroviral Therapy Programme at the University of Zimbabwe, which is now looking after my health. They have helped me to start and run a business. I can now look after my children and my finance is better. They have helped me forgive my husband for passing this virus to me and I feel strengthened that I am closer to Jesus Christ.

I have learnt to eat for health. I eat wholesome, unrefined foods and natural, unprocessed foods. I drink four litres of boiled water everyday. I enjoy the traditional foods of Zimbabwe and I even sell them to people who are having the same problem as me.

The Zimbabwe Parents of Children with Disabilities Association (ZPCDA), Harare Branch

Formed in 1987, the ZPCDA has practically contributed to the scaling-up of the livelihoods of children with disabilities in the country. The association was registered as a welfare organisation in 1990, with the help of Harare Hospital. Through their intervention, parents of children with disabilities have attended therapy sessions at Harare Hospital Children's Rehabilitation Unit (CRU).

Further, the programme has contributed immeasurably in the area of community-based rehabilitation, networking, childcare, stimulation activities, staff development, communication, publicity, HIV and AIDS awareness, lobbying and advocacy, grassroots capacity-building, gender-sensitisation and income-generating projects. Our Rehabilitation Outreach Team advised the mothers to organise themselves into a support group that unites parents and is a strong voice in lobbying for better services. We do not have the exact statistics of disabled children in Harare. CRU estimates that there are well over 3 000 disabled children living in high-density areas. Efforts have been made through the Ministries of Health, Education and Social Welfare to rehabilitate children with disabilities but a lot of constraints are being encountered.

Many families are marginalised because of cultural beliefs surrounding disability and do not get the support from the extended family. Most of our members are single mothers whose husbands have gone away because they have a disabled child. Most of these are living in difficult circumstances, as low-income lodgers, or widows. Research indicates that the risk of HIV infection is 2–4 times higher for women than men. AIDS can have a serious economic effect on the lives of women when it strikes a family member. Most women have no secure occupation, but this is worse for the mothers of the ZPCDA. Many have no rights of inheritance due to ignorance. Thus, if the husband dies, the surviving wife and children can be particularly vulnerable and subject to exploitation.

An AIDS orphan is defined as a child less than 15 years old who has lost parents to AIDS. A disabled AIDS orphan is even more disadvantaged, as relatives are not willing to take on a disabled child. Orphanages are not willing to take disabled children, and, moreover, do not have facilities to care for them. One of our members is fostering a disabled orphan.

The mothers of the ZPCDA assist each other and even look after children of fellow members. Most members live in the high-density suburbs. Those who are lucky enough to have jobs tend to work in the low-income bracket in the informal sector. Many have no income and live in rented accommodation. With the deteriorating economic condition of the country, state assistance is diminishing fast. The cost of living has risen drastically and many are finding it increasingly more difficult to support their families.

Disability, poverty and HIV
The struggles of mothers of disabled children

THERESA MAKWARA
Coordinator, ZPCDA, Harare Branch
Interview by Kaori Izumi, February 2005

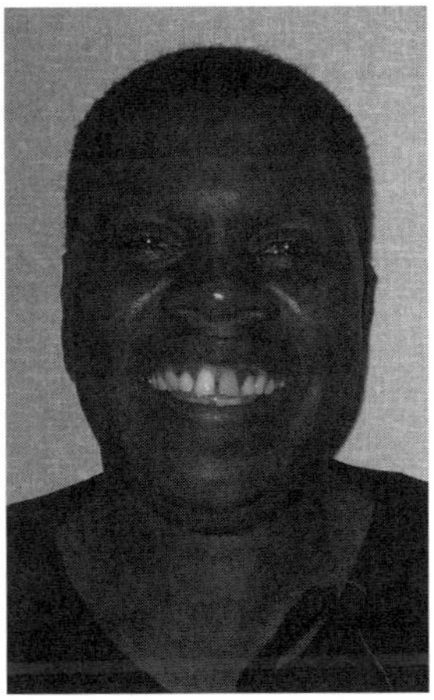

My name is Theresa Makwara. I am 38 years old. I live in my parents' house in Glen Norah, Harare. I used to live with my old parents, who are chronically ill, and my elder brother, who has a psychiatric problem. I was looking after them. I was divorced in 1991 because my husband thought I would have another disabled child. I have two children, aged 17 and 13, both boys. The eldest is disabled. He suffers from cerebral palsy due to asphyxia during his birth. My disabled son cannot walk or talk and he is in a wheelchair. He is at Ruvimbo School in Southerton. My other son is healthy and does not suffer from any problems of that nature.

My husband was a policeman and we were staying at Tomlison Depot when I delivered my first son at Harare Hospital. I met my husband when I joined the police force during my training. After our disabled son was born, it took six months for me to understand that my child had a disability. This was because the doctor had never explained it to me. It was his constant crying, lack of appetite and his inability to sit down that brought his disability to my attention. The doctor told me that the child and I were HIV-positive without even testing us. He emphasised that the child might die at any time and he was a useless child. We were referred to another specialist, who told us that our child had brain damage and that he needed physiotherapy. That was when we were referred to the Children's Rehabilitation Department. I was then invited to attend a workshop for parents with cerebral palsy at Harare Hospital Children's Rehabilitation Unit.

I gradually accepted the disability of my son. While I was busy looking after him, my husband started going out with other women. My husband destroyed all my school certificates, which I can never forgive him for. He later married another woman. The possibility that he may father another disabled child disturbed him to the point that he eventually became mentally unstable and committed suicide.

I am a member of the ZPCDA. I started in 1993 with the organisation, being one of the first members to lobby for the organisation. I was one of the activists. Today, we have over 400 members from Harare, out of which only 20 are fathers and the majority are single mothers. Our major objective is to improve the lives of children with disabilities, to empower the parents, to fight for the rights of our children, and to lobby and advocate. We have a parent-to-parent support programme and relief care through taking turns to look after one another's children. We have seven centres of our own and 16 groups. We have income-generating activities, such as drying bananas, and some of our mothers' groups make cards for sale. Some of our mothers are trained as enumerators and others in catering. Many of them do not have much of an education or skills, but we are working hard to support ourselves and our children. Our organisation has been struggling with funding. We used to get some support to pay salaries for the other mothers who were regular staff, but since January and February this year our resources have been exhausted, and we have been unable to pay salaries.

We have lost up to 20 members from our group to HIV and AIDS since 2003, though most did not disclose their status. We did some HIV and AIDS awareness for our members just before the FAO workshop on HIV and AIDS, Women's Property Rights and Livelihoods in Zimbabwe in December 2004. We discovered that a number of our members were living with problems of property-grabbing by relatives. They were also HIV-positive, and at the same time they had disabled children. We have never accessed funds from the National AIDS Council, although we tried some times but to no avail. We have lost more than 20 children since 2003. Some of the children were HIV-positive, including Peter. He was nine years old. Both of his parents had passed away and his mother's relatives were looking after him. Peter died last December. Another boy, George[17], was ten years old and died on 28 January 2005. George's mother was HIV-positive and she died in November 2004. She was a very active mother in our association, but she did not disclose her status. The mother's sister took over the care of George but, when she got pregnant, she sent George to relatives in Hurungwe in the rural areas. He was a disabled child and was not able to sit on his own. So they put him in a tyre. He spent whole days in there. He later died of bedsores, just a couple of months after he had been sent to the village.

The majority of the parents with disabled children are single mothers who were abandoned by their husbands when a disabled child was born. Other mothers lost their husband to HIV and AIDS, and they too are HIV-positive. I suspect that the infection rate among mothers with disabled children is higher than the mothers with 'normal' children. Mothers with disabled children are poorer; they cannot find jobs because they are uneducated and they have nobody to look after their disabled child. As a result, they look for men who can help them and they are infected in the process. We have not been able to systematically sensitise mothers of disabled children on HIV and AIDS because of lack of resources, and this is one of the priorities in our future programme.

Recently we found out that one 19-year-old disabled girl child was sexually abused by her own brother and his friends. The abuse took place at her home in Kambuzuma. Her mother had died and the father had remarried. The father later died. The girl and her brother stayed with her stepmother.

The girl is 19 and she is a child with learning difficulties. The sexual abuse by her brother and his friends has been happening since last year. Although we were told that the school had reported the case to the police and that it is in court, the process has been taking too long. We had a meeting with the headmistress on this issue. There are at least three such cases of sexual abuse concerning disabled girls in the same school. Another girl was impregnated; she opted to abort. The case was referred to the Family Support Unit at Harare Hospital, but nobody knows who had abused the child. The girl is 19 years old. I think these cases should be reported. But there is nobody who is actually standing up for this issue and we are the ones who are following the case.

We have five mothers whose property was grabbed by relatives and among them there are HIV-positive mothers and mothers with children with disabilities. The first mother gave her testimony at the FAO workshop on HIV and AIDS and Women's Property Rights in December 2004. The husband was a businessman in Domboshava. They had shops in a village. She approached the courts so many times and she never won anything. She was lucky – after the FAO workshop, the relatives surrendered the land and the property in the village.

In another case, the relatives took everything and the disabled child died. In the third case, relatives again took everything after the death of the husband. They were also from Domboshava. In a fourth case, the husband's relatives are threatening to move her out of the house where she is staying with her child in Mbare.

'Our children, howeve disabled, have the san rights as other childre

Parents of one of our disabled children were living positively with HIV. The father was in a camp. When the husband died, the mother and her two children were evicted from the camp. She was living in a plastic house for some time with her disabled child. We fought very hard to get a piece of land from the Municipal Office and she managed to build a house with the husband's pension. But later she died of HIV and AIDS. The disabled child is living with his brother who is a teacher, together with a housemaid who looks after the child.

When my son was born, I was crying every day because I thought that I was bewitched by some relatives. This is common belief in Zimbabwe that you deliver a disabled child because somebody has bewitched you. It took some time for me to understand that it was not witchcraft. As a result, people do not like disabled children.

We are determined to fight for the rights of these women and our children. Our children, however disabled, have the same rights as other children. The community should be taught about these issues so that women can live in peace and harmony. The government should support more programmes like ours.

The Farm Orphan Support Trust of Zimbabwe (FOST)

FOST was established in 1997 and is working to reduce the impact and mitigate the effects of HIV and AIDS on children and young people in farm communities and to create an environment where all children can grow and develop to their full potential. The long-term objective of FOST is to proactively increase the capacity of farm worker communities to respond to the orphan crisis. The current situation in farming areas has, however, necessitated the development of short-term objectives linked to emergency needs of orphans and vulnerable children (OVC) in these communities.

FOST programmes include:

- Community awareness-raising and advocacy on child protection and children's rights (including inheritance and property rights);
- Education assistance and psychosocial support targeting children affected and infected by HIV and AIDS, especially orphans;
- Child supplementary feeding for children and pregnant mothers;
- Material and psychosocial support for the households affected by HIV and AIDS, especially child-head households;
- Home-based care;
- 'Kids Clubs', where older children offer support for each other and younger children;
- Child protection, and livelihoods training for out-of-school OVC.

Currently, FOST is supporting over 7000 OVC through school (over 50 per cent girls) and supplying child supplementary feeding for 23 000 children. The organisation has a network of over 500 volunteers in the farm communities of Manicaland and Mashonaland Central.

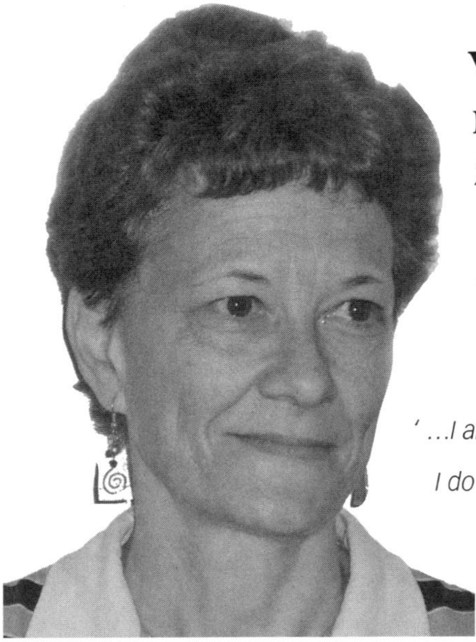

Women without property
Female farm workers in Zimbabwe

LYNN WALKER
Executive Director (2000–2005), FOST

'...I am an 18-year-old girl in Form 3 at a secondary school. I do not have the fees for this year and the headmaster at school is telling me I must go home unless I find the money for the fees. I live with my two brothers who are aged 16 and 12. Our mother was a farm worker and she died last year. We have no one to look after us. I never knew my father. The man who was my older brother's father died in 2000. My mother married another man who is very sick and is staying with his relatives. He is the father of the last-born. The family will not take us because they say my mother made him sick. We do not know if the other father had any relatives ...'

This extract from a letter from Sekai illustrates not only how children in farm communities are affected by the AIDS pandemic, but also how the situation of women in these communities increases their vulnerability to HIV infection and AIDS.

Sekai's mother, a casual worker for many years on a commercial farm near Harare, had a number of sexual partners during her short life. Not because she was a sex worker, but because, for her, the best chance she had of a stable and secure life was to form a relationship with a man who had a permanent position at the farm. She is typical of many women farm workers who are not permanently employed and, hence, have no security and few rights.

Traditionally, women farm workers were rarely given permanent positions on farms because they were perceived as being prone to absenteeism due to sick children and pregnancy. Some women workers were the wives or daughters of permanently employed men, but many were single women, often with children, who are attracted to farm work through lack of alternatives. Farm work gave women an opportunity to raise money for school fees, uniforms and health care and in some cases provided food, housing and schooling, if only temporarily.

Despite this, until the upheavals around the land reform process, women formed the bulk of the workforce. In 1999, the Central Statistical Office figures showed that only 9.7 per cent of all permanent farm workers were women and that the majority of women on farms were employed as seasonal or casual workers. The Farm Community Trust of Zimbabwe said that in 2002 over 55 per cent of contract workers on farms were women and that women made up approximately one third of all farm workers. Of all households on farms at this time, 19 per cent were headed by females.

Being a 'contract' worker, however, means that there is no right to permanent accommodation, sick leave, vacation leave, health and maternity benefits, pension or gratuities. Where a farm is acquired for resettlement, they do not receive terminal benefits or retrenchment packages. In addition, women farm workers engaged in casual or seasonal work rarely have the opportunity to receive training that would enable then to rise to more skilled jobs or supervisory positions which would make them permanent workers.

Women with Zimbabwean roots, working on a seasonal or casual basis, may have a rural home to go to at the end of their contract. For these women, farm work is a way to enhance the economic strength of the family and often their children and property remain in their rural home. Many farm women, however, are descended from people who migrated to Zimbabwe, often two or three generations ago, and who have no ancestral roots to fall back on. They have no access to land in their own right, own little real property and have no safety net in times of crisis. Illness, drought, a cyclone, land reform or pregnancy can all mean that there is no longer work for them and they lose everything.

This 'inferior' status and vulnerability frequently leads them into casual relationships with men, when promised 'marriage'. This may represent their only chance for a recognised 'home' and a secure future. Where women form such a relationship, however, it is rarely formalised and often unstable. Sometimes the relationship may last only as long as the season and when contract work is finished, the women find that the liaison is also at an end. Even where the relationship endures longer, once it is over, any children from the 'marriage' are not recognised by the father or his family and so the children move on with their mother. If the mother dies, this can leave the children unacknowledged and unsupported. The following case of Tatenda and Susan[18] illustrates this.

Tatenda, who is 12, and his 8-year-old sister Susan first came to FOST's attention in 2002, a year after their mother died. They never knew their father and no one in the community was aware of who their real father was. Their mother, a Mozambican, was known to have worked on three farms in the vicinity and to have 'married' a different man on each farm. When FOST approached the families of these men, however, none would acknowledge the paternity of the children and the 'husbands' were either deceased or living with another partner. The neighbours also knew nothing about the mother or her family and were unable to help FOST trace any maternal relatives. When their mother died, the two children were left with few possessions – some basic household items and their clothing. The mother left behind no furniture or goods and no documentation to help the children trace their extended family. Tatenda and Susan were lucky because, in general, the house itself would not be tied to the job, but in this case the owner allowed them to remain in the house indefinitely.

HIV and AIDS have exacerbated this vulnerability of women farm workers and further illustrate the impoverished and powerless state of so many farm women and their dependent children. In some cases, women farm workers are forced to engage in sexual relationships with men in supervisory or management positions in order to obtain and keep work. These 'carpet interviews' often leave the women vulnerable to sexually transmitted infections, HIV infection or pregnancy.

In December 2000, the Ministry of Health found that the HIV prevalence rate amongst farm and mine communities was 54 per cent. In the same year, the Bio-Medical Research and Training Institute found that 15 per cent of men and 27 per cent of women on estates in Mutasa district were HIV-positive. In farming areas in Nyazura this figure went up to 29 per cent and 44 per cent, respectively. The same research found that the peak ages for new infections were the mid-20s for men and the late teens for women. This indicates that farm communities are disproportionably affected by HIV and that women in farm communities are more vulnerable to HIV infection than men.

Enumeration data from FOST has shown, however, that although women are more vulnerable to HIV infection they are the main caregivers for sick adults and for orphaned children in farm communities and form the bulk of community volunteers. In 2003, nearly 60 per cent of all orphaned children enumerated by FOST had lost their father and only 25 per cent had lost their mother only. The same figures showed that over 60 per cent of all households with orphaned and vulnerable children (OVC) were female-headed.

This illustrates how, despite their susceptibility to abuse and exploitation and the challenges of their lives, farm women are still able to show resilience and the capacity to support the most disadvantaged in their communities. Despite the lack of value placed upon their work and their social worth, farm women contribute enormously to the social capital of farm communities. On some farms this had been recognised and, prior to the recent upheavals around the land reform programme, many established farmers, especially in horticultural enterprises, were offering increasing numbers of permanent positions to women.

As one women farm worker said: 'They say they are men's jobs, but I ask why? I can do any of the jobs these men do … After work I go home and give the benefit to my children. You will not find me drinking my money at the bar … '

Afterword

KAORI IZUMI

During the past years, slow but positive development has taken place with regards to women's land and property rights. At the national level, follow-up activities for the Secretary General's initiative have been initiated and a national plan for action to implement the recommendations of a national report is being drafted in some of the countries, that is, Zambia, Malawi and Zimbabwe.

In 2004, the Centre for Housing Rights and Evictions (COHRE), the Huairou Commission, UN-HABITAT and FAO have set up a project called Women Land Link Africa, funded by SIDA. The primary objectives of the project are:

- Mapping and setting up a database on organisations and activities on women's housing, land and property rights in the Africa region;
- Documenting grassroots women's group's initiatives to secure women's housing, land and property rights and facilitating exchanges among them.

As a follow-up to the Secretary General's Special Committee on Women, Girls and HIV and AIDS in Southern Africa, a joint initiative has been taken by the UN and civil society organisations. A Global Coalition on AIDS and Women's Property Rights was co-convened by the International Centre for Research on Women (ICRW) and FAO. The first partners' meeting was held in Nairobi in January 2005, involving key UN agencies and civil society organisations, including grassroots organisations from the region. The Coalition has identified two major priority areas:

- Domesticating international legal standards on women's property rights into national laws;
- Mobilising resources and to supporting grassroots groups working on HIV and AIDS and women's property rights.

The ICRW together with the Global Coalition has successfully secured funds from UNAIDS to set up a small grants initiative to support grassroots organisations on HIV and AIDS and women's property rights. As I write this conclusion, a selection of proposals is on-going for the first disbursement of these funds.

The latest positive development is that the inclusion of women's ownership of property and housing and inheritance laws has made its way into the Revised Draft Outcome Document of the High-Level Plenary Meeting of the UN General Assembly of September 2005. Paragraph 58, under 'Gender Equality and Empowerment of Women', stated:

The full and effective implementation of the Beijing Declaration and Platform for Action is essential to achieving the internationally agreed development goals, including those contained in the Millennium Declaration; and to promote gender equality and to eliminate pervasive gender discrimination (among others) by:

- *Guaranteeing the right of women to property, housing and inheritance laws and ensuring secure tenure of property and housing to women;*[19]
- *Ensuring equal access to women to productive assets and resources, including land, credit and technology.*

A real challenge before us is how the new Millennium Development Goals, new laws and policies, networks, knowledge and projects will actually change the lives of the women and children, including those who have testified in this book.

Endnotes

1 Anna Ngonge was a member of Mathere home-based care group in Kenya and died on 13 March 2004. Her narrative is included in this book. Precious Kyarisima was the youngest member of Bunono-Ihunga Women's Association for Women Living with HIV and AIDS in Rukungiri, Uganda. She died in October 2004.

2 According to UNDP Human Development Report, the date refers to 2002 data, whereas World Facts and Figures May 2004 shows that the GDP per capita for Zimbabwe for 2002 is US$ 1,900 (Wold Facts and Figures, DGP Capita, 11 May 2004).

3 This introduction does not reflect the views of the Food and Agricultural Organisation (FAO) of the United Nations and the author is solely responsible for all the views expressed herein. It is based on two presentations, namely the opening speech at a national workshop on 'HIV and AIDS, Women's Property Rights and Livelihoods in Zimbabwe', which was held in Harare on 1–2 December 2004, and a presentation at a Livelihoods Support Programme seminar at FAO in Rome held on 10 December 2004.

4 This is a pseudonym.

5 The prevalent culture in Eritrea discourages women from ploughing by disseminating superstitious views that crops do not grow on the land ploughed by women and that if a woman winnows the produce, it will be blown away by the wind (Zerai 2001).

6 UNDP (2001), citing 1999 figures. Adults imply the age group between 15–49 and children implies 0–14 years old.

7 This is a pseudonym.

8 *Safari* means journey in Swahili.

9 *Shamba* means farming plot in Swahili.

10 Beatrice Wanjiru Muguiyi is not formally divorced, but evicted and abandoned by her husband.

11 This is a pseudonym.

12 Stephen Lewis is the UN Special Envoy on HIV and AIDS.

13 The reason the daughters could inherit his land at his rural home was because the girls would marry elsewhere and leave the village one day, therefore leaving the land to his family.

14 *Sibabinyewere* means tied together.

15 Mrs Chilala testified at a national workshop on HIV and AIDS and women's property rights in Zimbabwe in December 2004. Although this case is not related to HIV and AIDS, it is an extreme case of the violation of human rights and property rights of women in Zambia today.

16 Chapter 37 is a civil marriage.

17 Peter and George are pseudonyms.

18 Tatenda and Susan are pseudonyms.

19 The draft resolution referred to the High-Level Plenary Meeting of the General Assembly by the General Assembly at its fifty-ninth session, 2005 World Summit Outcome, adopted on 16 September 2005, United Nations.

References

Bosworth J (2002) Integrating land issues into the broader development agenda: Uganda country case study. Paper presented at the Regional Workshop on Land Issues in Africa, Kampala (29 April to 2 May 2002)

BRTI (2000) *Bio-medical Research and Training Institute Epidemic Status Report: Zimbabwe*. Harare: Manicaland HIV/STD Prevention Project, BRTI.

COHRE (2004) *Bringing Equality Home: Promoting and Protecting the Inheritance Rights of Women – A Survey of Law and Practice in Sub-Saharan Africa.* Geneva: The Centre on Housing Rights and Evictions.

Dodo AT (2003) Venia Magaya's Sacrifice: A case of custom gone awry. Paper presented at the FAO/OXFAM GB workshop on women's land rights in Southern And Eastern Africa. Pretoria (17-19 June 2003). Accessed April 2006, http://www.oxfam.org.uk/what_we_do/issues/livelihoods/landrights/downloads/wlrseareport.doc

FAO (2003a) *National Draft Strategy: Kenya.* Rome: FAO.

FAO (2003b) *Agricultural Sector Brief: South Africa.* Rome: FAO.

FAO (2003c) *Draft National Strategy 2015: Swaziland.* Rome: FAO.

FAO (2003d) *Agricultural Brief Draft: Uganda*. Rome: FAO.

FAO (2003e) *Zambia Strategy Brief for Food Security and Agricultural Development.* Rome: FAO.

FAO (2005a) *Aquastat: South Africa.* Accessed April 2006, http://www.fao.org/ag/agl/aglw/aquastat/countries/south_africa/index.stm

FAO (2005b) *Aquastat: Swaziland.* Accessed April 2006, http://www.fao.org/ag/agl/aglw/aquastat/countries/swaziland/index.stm

FAO (2005c) *Aquastat: Zimbabwe.* Accessed April 2006,http://www.fao.org/ag/agl/aglw/aquastat/countries/zimbabwe/index.stm

Ikdahl I, Hellum A, Kaarhus R, Benjaminsen TA, Kameri-Mbote P (2005) Human rights, formalisation and women's land rights in southern and eastern Africa. In *Studies in Women's Law 57*. Oslo: Institute of Women's Law, University of Oslo. Accessed April 2006, http://www.sarpn.org.za/documents/d0001447/index.php

OXFAM GB (2004) Land reform highlights in eastern Africa, 2003-4. *Independent Land Newsletter* August 2004. Oxford: OXFAM GB

Save the Children UK (2005) Country brief 2004/5: Tanzania. Accessed April 2006, http://www.savethechildren.org.uk/cb/Tanz.pdf

Shakafuswa F (2004) Chikuni Tribunal was an eye opener, *The JWOP News.* Issue no. 1, January–March 2004. Lusaka: JWOP

Subramanian J (1996) Eritrea Country Profile. In JW Bruce *Country Profiles of Land Tenure: Africa*, 1996. Madison: Land Tenure Centre, University of Wisconsin-Madison. Accessed April 2006, http://www.ies.wisc.edu/ltc/rp130.html

TACAIDS (n.d.) *HIV/AIDS in Tanzania*. Accessed April 2006, http://www.tanzania.go.tz/hiv_aids.html

Tsehainesh T (1998) Women's access to land and property rights in Eritrea. *Women's Land and Property Rights in Situations of Conflict and Reconstruction*. Accessed April 2006, http://oxfam.co.uk/what_we_do/issues/livelihoods/landrights/downloads/eritprop.rtf

Tibaijuka, AK (2005) *UN-HABITAT Report of Operation Murambatsvina by the UN Special Envoy on Human Settlement Issues in Zimbabwe*. Accessed April 2006, http://www.un.org/News/dh/infocus/zimbabwe/zimbabwe_rpt.pdf

UNAIDS (2004) *2004 Report on the global AIDS epidemic*. Accessed April 2006, http://www.unaids.org/bangkok2004/GAR2004_html/GAR2004_00_en.htm

UNDP (2001) *Addressing social and economic disparities for human development. Human Development Report: Kenya, 2001*. Accessed April 2006, http://www.ke.undp.org/Human%20Developement%20Report%202001.pdf

UNDP (2003) *UNDP Zimbabwe Human Development Report 2003: Redirecting our responses to HIV and AIDS*. Accessed April 2006, http://hdr.undp.org/docs/reports/national/ZIM_Zimbabwe/Zimbabwe_2003_en.pdf

UNDP (2005) *International cooperation at a crossroads: Aid, trade and security in an unequal world. Human Development Report 2005*. Accessed April 2006, http://hdr.undp.org/reports/global/2005/

UN-HABITAT (2002) *Rights and Reality: Are women's equal rights to land, housing and property implemented in East Africa?* Accessed April 2006, http://www.unhabitat.org/publication/hs66702e/default.asp

US Department of State (2006) *Background note: Rwanda*. Accessed April 2006, http://www.state.gov/r/pa/ei/bgn/2861.htm

Walker C (2002) *Land Reform in Southern and Eastern Africa: Key issues for strengthening women's access to and rights in land.* Report on a desktop study commissioned by the Food and Agricultural Organization (FAO) (FAO Sub-regional office for Southern and Eastern Africa, Harare, Zimbabwe). Accessed April 2006, http://www.oxfam.org.uk/what_we_do/issues/livelihoods/landrights/downloads/accessrtf.rtf

WLSA (1997) *Women and Law in Southern Africa*. Harare: Women and Law in Southern Africa Research Trust.

WLSA (2001) *Critical analysis of women's access to land in the WLSA countries*. Harare: Women and Law in Southern Africa Research Trust.

World Bank (1995) *Swaziland Household Income and Expenditure Survey*. Accessed April 2006, http://www4.worldbank.org/afr/poverty/databank/survnav/show_survey.cfm?ID=46&page=docu

Zerai W (2001) *Women and land in Eritrea*. Accessed April 2006, http://www.eassi.org/uploaded_files/1075279216eritrea_report.pdf